D1247602

IDEAS IN MOTION

THE APPLETON–CENTURY
HISTORICAL ESSAYS

EDITED BY
WILLIAM E. LINGELBACH

———

VOLUMES PUBLISHED

SOURCES OF CULTURE IN THE MIDDLE
WEST, edited by Dixon Ryan Fox

IDEAS IN MOTION, by Dixon Ryan Fox

VOLUMES ARRANGED FOR

DEMOCRACY AND DICTATORSHIP,
by Robert Clarkson Brooks, William E.
Lingelbach, Ernest M. Patterson.

The Appleton=Century Historical Essays
WILLIAM E. LINGELBACH, Editor

IDEAS IN MOTION

BY

DIXON RYAN FOX

D. APPLETON–CENTURY COMPANY
INCORPORATED

New York   *London*

FOREWORD

AN author's foreword is likely to be either a boast or a disclaimer. To publish a book at all is a boast that one has something to say, and to publish a slight little book with a somewhat pompous title might imply a ridiculous boast. The author therefore begs the reader's patience for one preliminary moment to explain that his only intention is to suggest a few threads which might be considered in designing a history of the American people, threads so important that they might, to some extent, govern a not inconsiderable part of the pattern. The reader will protest, quite sensibly, that he would prefer a finished fabric to a few bright threads. So would the author. But since a multi-volume masterpiece is not likely to proceed from his hand, because of personal deficiencies and, recently, the scholarly disadvantages of an administrative post, it seemed defensible, even desirable, to put together these four papers as illustrations of certain approaches to American history which apparently have been neglected. *The American Historical Review* has kindly permitted the inclusion of two essays previously printed in its pages; but each has been revised and expanded.

DIXON RYAN FOX

Union College

CONTENTS

PAGE

CIVILIZATION IN TRANSIT 3

CULTURE IN KNAPSACKS 37

A SYNTHETIC PRINCIPLE IN AMERICAN SOCIAL
    HISTORY 77

REFUSE IDEAS AND THEIR DISPOSAL 99

IDEAS IN MOTION

CIVILIZATION IN TRANSIT

ABOUT thirty-five years ago Edward Eggleston published a volume whose title set the reader thinking before he turned the cover, *The Transit of Civilization from England to America in the Seventeenth Century*. Americans, then, did not invent their culture, but had to bring its elements from Europe bit by bit, however much they might be modified by transplantation. The thoughtful reader, setting side by side before his mind's eye a picture of the shaggy wilderness the colonists had to conquer and that of the age-old communities they had left behind, might readily presume that, though the individuals were hardly conscious of it, the process which the book would trace was neither short nor simple. What Eggleston considered was not the fundamental economic problem of staying alive in a new country, but the saving and carrying forward of arts and sciences, those refinements and specializations which come from intelligently living together. The transit, quite obviously, was not completed in the seventeenth century, nor is it yet complete; and when a given institution or practice reached the western shores of the Atlantic it yet had

[3]

far to go. Few men could have realized this more vividly than Eggleston himself, who had spent the years of his young manhood as a circuit rider in southern Indiana and the farther West and been a herald and exemplar of civilization in the backwoods.

Much has been written of the man with the axe, slowly cutting back the forest, fighting off malaria and mortgages as well as wild beasts and Indians and horse-thieves and establishing American ideals of energy and self-reliance. These men and women of the cabin did the basic work; they cleared the way and built foundations. At the beginning of the nineteenth century they constituted more than nine-tenths of our population. But if all had been of this type who made their way across the sea and across American hills and valleys it would have taken many centuries to build a great civilization. In their wake followed pioneers of ideas and special competence, quite as brave and worthy. As the woodsman-farmer with his axe and hoe took a risk, as to whether untamed nature would let him live, so these men with the book, the scalpel, the compass, to say nothing of the microscope and test-tube, took a risk, as to whether the social soil was deep and rich enough to sustain their specialties. How professional competence was transplanted to America makes an interesting study.

[4]

Let us begin with a well-known figure, the family doctor. The herbalists and leeches who came over during the first century were certainly not highly skilled, even when they made healing the sick their chief concern and not merely a side-line of the Christian ministry. But their obvious usefulness at last stirred certain native youth to equal or surpass them, not through mere apprenticeship but by resort to the original sources of instruction in Europe. In 1734 young William Bull, of Charles Town, returned with his M.D. from the University of Leyden, and six years later Isaac Dubois, of New York, could claim the same distinction; during the thirty-five years that followed scores of young men undertook the arduous journey with the same ambition, most of them taking up their study in Edinburgh. Two so graduated, Drs. William Shippen and John Morgan, returned to Philadelphia in the seventeen-sixties prepared to set up formal courses of instruction. "The time was ripe," and from their efforts grew the medical school of that city, soon rivalled by a second at King's College in New York. In both cases the staff was largely of British training and the methods closely imitative, even to the printed doctor's thesis, oftentimes in Latin, solemnly defended before the assembled faculty. In time it was loudly boasted, and finally believed, that one might become a first-rate

[5]

doctor without going to Europe, and by the early years of the nineteenth century these and other medical schools were staffed with their own product. It had taken about two centuries to transfer medical science to America.

The major phenomena of the transit are well illustrated by this type example. Four stages are discerned: first, when foreign practitioners of the specialty are received by the pioneer community; second, when the native youth go to the old country to attend upon instruction; third, when institutions of the special learning are established in the new land, though still dependent on the metropolis for the equipment of their teachers; fourth, when the institutions have sufficiently developed to maintain themselves.

He who applies this key to others of the older professional specialties will be surprised to see how well it works. It enables us to see the present stage of transit in various concerns. In great music we are still to a considerable degree in the first stage— so obviously true is this that certain *virtuosi* sprung from old American village stock, like Mme. Nordica, Ricardo Martin and Richard Bonnelli, have thought it added to their personal prestige to Europeanize their names. Scarcely thirty years ago when Richard Conried planned to produce John Knowles Paine's opera *Azara* at the Metropolitan

he had to give up his plan because no basso or con-
tralto could be found in the company who could
sing well enough in English to take the leading
rôles. Thomas Hastings, born in Connecticut and
reared in New York State, became one of America's leading hymnologists, producing more than a
thousand tunes, some of them of classic standing.
But in the middle of the nineteenth century he well
knew the value of a European pose. "I have
found," said he, "that a foreigner's name went a
great way, and that very ordinary tunes would be
sung if 'Palestrina' or 'Pucitto' were written over
them, while a better tune by Hastings would go un-
noticed." In pictorial and plastic art we are emerging from the second stage into the third. In university scholarship we reached the fourth stage only at
the end of the last century; it was not long ago that
a German Ph.D. was deemed highly important, if
not essential, to a first-class professor. But now
there is some evidence that in this concern we are
reversing the process to the second stage. When in
1815 Edward Everett matriculated at a German
university he blazed the way for more than ten
thousand Americans during the nineteenth century. To-day the tide has turned, and there are at
this moment more than ten thousand foreign students attending our universities, twice the number
of Americans now studying in foreign countries. In

[7]

architecture, in some forms of applied science and perhaps in business organization we have already registered this achievement, and in dentistry we have reversed the process even to the third stage.

After these reflections we may, perhaps, propose a generalization applicable to the normal conditions of modern history: professional competence rises through provincial to metropolitan status by the process of reception, attendance, dependent organization, and self-maintenance. If we were to stifle our sense of humor we might even call this a "law." At least it has the two major requisites of a sociological law, in that when baldly stated it is so ponderously cryptic as to be unintelligible, and when explained it is so obvious that it need not have been stated at all.

It must be understood that in this use of the word "provincial" there is no reference of necessity to political dependence. Metropolis and province may change places without regard to politics; ideas flowed from France into England in the Norman days, and from England into France during the first half of the eighteenth century. Sometimes, indeed, the victors adopt the culture of their victims, as when in the phrase of Horace:

Greece, conquered Greece, her conquerors subdued
And clownish Latium with her arts imbued.

[8]

The importation of culture has oftentimes been artificially stimulated by autocrats—assumption by fiat—as is recalled by mention of the names of Peter the Great and Mustapha Kemal, to say nothing of the ministers of Mutsuhito. And the export has been stimulated quite as well. Christian missions have been a most important agency in carrying secular culture abroad as well as religious, if, indeed, the two can be sharply distinguished. Many patriotic Frenchmen, for example, who believe the Catholic faith a silly superstition contribute to its propagation beyond the seas, proud that "backward areas" are thus becoming Gallicized. Publications of hyphenate societies supported at least in part from the old home-land abound in many places. But the process has worked normally without artificial aid. Cataclysms may stimulate it, as when in the seventeen-nineties the *émigrés* from France and Santo Domingo brought French opera, cotillions, and fine cooking to America. Dr. Samuel Latham Mitchill, in a discourse delivered in 1821 at Union College, declared that European wars had been the cause of a quickened transit of books from the Old World to the New, that some distinguished refugees had brought their libraries, that booksellers, deprived of markets at home, had brought their stocks in increasing number: "The storm from the east has wafted, in short, an abundance of precious

[9]

things to these regions." But, again, the process can not be generally explained as a concomitant of great disturbance in the metropolis.

The operation in particulars, indeed, seems strikingly accidental, and this not only in the professions but in the trades as well, where, of course, the first stage merges directly into the last. Naturalists tell us that in the islands of the South Sea the wind and flying birds carry spores and seeds from one land-area to another, where if the soil conditions are propitious a plant springs up and a part of the flora is thus reproduced beyond the water. Almost as fortuitous seem the circumstances by which carriers of civilization have been transferred to America.

Take, for example, the case of Samuel Slater, in 1789 an apprentice spinner in the employ of Richard Arkwright's partner in Belper, England. Learning by chance at the age of twenty-one, when his term of service had expired, that there was some curiosity in America as to Arkwright's patents, he resolved to try his fortune overseas. But the statute of 22 George III., chapter 60, framed according to old mercantilist doctrine, forbade the taking out of England of any machinery, models, or mechanical drawings and, indeed, the migration of artisans. So young Slater by a feat of concentration memorized the entire series of wheels and bands and rollers with precise dimensions and, disguised as a countryman, slipped by the English customs officers without their once suspecting the illicit cargo that he carried in his mind. On arriving in New York he heard that Moses Brown, a Rhode Island Quaker, had made some trials at cotton spinning, and wrote him a letter setting forth what he could do. The answer came quite promptly: "If thee canst do this thing, I invite thee to come to Rhode Island, and have the credit of introducing cotton manufacture into America." Thereupon he went to Pawtucket, the one most fortunate place in the country, where waterwheels and ships were found within the same small town, and there he built his frames and did become what Moses Brown had prophesied. The seed had landed on good soil.

It is somewhat puzzling to the reader of industrial statistics to account for the concentration of the brass manufacture in the Naugatuck Valley in Connecticut. There is neither copper, nor zinc, nor coal found in that vicinity, nor is it exceptionally well placed for transportation; why, then, should eighty-five per cent of America's brass be made there? The answer is, the accident of the carrier. In 1820 an artisan named Crofts left a Birmingham brass-works as an emigrant. On landing in America he drifted about and finally into Waterbury. Here he found some humble manufacturers making notions for tin-peddlers, among other things a few brass buttons from old copper kettles and ship bottoms and imported zinc. Hiring out as a hand he showed his new employers better methods, was made a partner, and was sent back to Birmingham some seven or eight times to recruit more skilled workers; on the basis of this skill the brass business was established.

If one works through the records of any branch of human effort in America, one comes upon these carriers, individual men and women more or less conscious of the function they perform. In 1805 one Ferdinand Rudolph Hassler came from Switzerland to Philadelphia, bringing with him some books and mathematical instruments. Through the good offices of Secretary Gallatin, his compatriot, and the interest of President Jefferson, he was given a place as a teacher at West Point, and thus brought the knowledge of analytical geometry to America; he advised the government as to a method of charting the coastal waters, was sent abroad to buy more instruments, and on his return began the United States Coast Survey. The man with the special competence had happened to meet the special need. About the same time, in 1816, there came to the military academy Claude Crozet, who had been schooled at the Polytechnique in Paris—and thus began the study of descriptive geometry in this country; having been an engineer under Napoleon and having had the severe training in higher mathematics that most of our practitioners sadly lacked, after seven years' teaching he became an employee of Virginia and gave the state a system of roads which made it for that time a model. This was the contribution of two Europeans to American mathematics. English books were usually the seeds of early American architecture, but there were human carriers too that we can recognize, like Richard Upjohn, who in 1829 brought to New England the ideas of the Gothic revival, later to flower in his Trinity Church in New York City. Similar stories could be told for almost every branch of art and science.

But some have transferred to the province parts of the metropolitan environment itself. In 1714 the ablest young thinkers of Connecticut were spinning out dry dichotomies of dry ideas—working knowledge out of their own heads, as the Reverend Samuel Johnson wrote in reminiscence. Then there came to Yale a library which Jeremy Dummer, the colonial agent, had sent from the old country, and for the first time New England came into contact with John Locke and Isaac Newton and modern thought. The effect, as Johnson writes of it, was sudden and tremendous; he himself and other clergymen left Calvinism and stirred the religious thinking of the Puritan colonies as it had not been stirred before—all because of a library. In 1796, or thereabouts, Dr. Adam Seybert, of Philadelphia, brought back from Europe a cabinet of minerals, the second in the country; it was to this collection that young Benjamin Silliman, of New Haven, brought a little box of stones for comparison and identification, and thus was started on his way to be the first great American master of geology, and it was the elaborate cabinet which Colonel George Gibbs brought across the water that aided Silliman to make Yale the center of such studies. In 1794 Dr. David Hosack returned with a duplicate collection of plants from the herbarium of Linnaeus, and shortly afterward brought in seeds, slips, and shrubs to form his botanical garden, specimens from which made up the core of the great establishment in Bronx Park; such new advantages made the study of botany by Americans a very different thing from what it had been before.

The fine art of Europe was started westward only when American wealth had sufficiently accumulated to secure it. There were collections as early as the seventeen-nineties, like that brought to Boston by James Swan, and that to Philadelphia by William Hamilton, but they had little cultural value while shut within a few private houses. It was not until the latter half of the nineteenth century, about

1870, to be exact, that private fortune seriously took up the task of educating the public taste by transferring European art to open galleries in this country. Notable collections of Italian primitives and other pieces were given to the New York Historical Society by Thomas Jefferson Bryan and to Yale by James J. Jarves; William W. Corcoran in 1869 endowed a museum in Washington to receive his importations; in 1870 one group of philanthropists organized the Museum of Fine Arts in Boston and another the Metropolitan Museum in New York City. Such benefactions though conspicuous for scale were not different in spirit from earlier and more modest transfers like that accomplished by Daniel Wadsworth and his associates for Hartford in 1842 and that by the Reverend A. W. Freeman who brought copies to the Indiana colleges in the 'sixties and 'seventies. By reason of such establishments artists could see something of the legacy of bygone centuries without leaving their own soil. The process was continued by Morgan, Frick, and a host of others, until now, apparently, American purchasers are so much the reliance of those who market the historic art of Europe that collections, like that of Lord Leverhulme, are moved here intact for the auctioneer. Thus, in the transit of civilization one factor has been the removal of environment itself.

[15]

The transit as a whole, apparently, was speeded by the Revolution, which for a time so developed the sentiment of nationalism that it irked us to depend on Europe for anything. The audience at the John Street Theatre, New York, on April 16, 1787, applauded the prologue of Royall Tyler's play, *The Contrast,* with its announcement of an innovation:

Exult each patriot heart—tonight is shewn
A piece which we may fairly call our own;
Where the proud titles of "My Lord! Your Grace!"
To humble Mr. and plain Sir give place.
Our author pictures not from foreign climes
The fashions or the follies of the times;
But has confin'd the subject of his work
To the gay scenes—the circles of New York.

In the introduction to her novel *Dorval, the Speculator* (1801), Madam Wood, of Portland, echoed the same sentiment: "Hitherto we have been indebted to France, Germany, and Great Britain, for the majority of our literary pleasures. Why we should not aim at independence, with respect to our mental enjoyments, as well as our more substantial gratifications, I know not. Why must the amusements of our leisure hours cross the Atlantic? . . . The following pages are wholly American; the characters are those of our own country."

The customary deference and dependence, it is true, were not easily thrown off. In colonial days many whose ancestors had lived here for a hundred years and who themselves had never left our shores still spoke wistfully of England as "home." William Dunlap, the leading theatrical manager at the beginning of the nineteenth century, was not a little irritated by the general distrust of American playwrights; *The Contrast* itself was none too successful. When in 1808 James Nelson Barker dramatized *Marmion,* his manager Wood feared to announce it to Philadelphia as of local workmanship. "The merit of the piece was positive," says Wood, "but the old difficulty remained. I knew the then prejudice against any native play, and concocted . . . a very innocent fraud upon the public. We insinuated that the piece was a London one, had it sent to our theatre from New York, where it was made to arrive in the midst of a rehearsal, in the presence of the actors, packed up exactly like the pieces we were in the habit of receiving from London. . . . It was played with great success for six or seven nights, when believing it safe I announced the author." The New York *Columbian,* praising a new play in 1819, was impressed with its own courage: "We advance this opinion without waiting for the fiat of an English audience, or an English review." Fenimore Cooper, the following year, did not dare confess the American authorship of his first novel and sent it out more safely as the work of an anonymous Englishwoman. The highest encomium his later admirers could pronounce was to call him the American Scott; many, however, thought this hardly in good taste, not because it indicated undue deference to British standards, but because the comparison seemed presumptuous. Nevertheless, the national consciousness was coming. Most Americans were extremely sensitive when British critics dismissed us as provincial. The bitter vehemence of C. J. Ingersoll, Robert Walsh, and J. K. Paulding, who tried to prove that we were not, was perhaps in itself a telling bit of evidence that we still were; but, for all that, there was a growing sentiment that it was time for Americans, even in concerns outside of government, to assume "the separate and equal station to which the Laws of Nature and of Nature's God entitled them."

The science of botany gives an interesting example. Since it did not reach the status of a specialized profession in Europe until far on in the nineteenth century, it cannot well be subjected to our "law." Yet it had an interesting process of its own in transition. First came European explorers, like Mark Catesby and Peter Kalm; then, somewhat overlapping, Americans who were the correspondents of great scholars in the old countries, such as John Clayton, who sent collections to Gronovius, and John Bartram, who supplied the English Quaker, Peter Collinson. But the amateur botanists of the United States, mostly doctors of medicine or of divinity, resented foreign domination, especially such European christening of American plants. "We ought," wrote the most distinguished of them, the Reverend H. E. Muhlenberg, in 1811, "we ought to be jealous for our American names. Why should we have the trouble of finding, and other nations the honor?" In this concern, as in many others, patriotism spurred us to catch up with Europe. Sometimes the cultural self-reliance was encouraged by the old country; the American Board of Commissioners for Foreign Missions (1810) and the American Bible Society (1816) were formed because English organizations not unnaturally refused to undertake the administration of American philanthropy. But generally the new nation insisted on becoming as free as possible in every way.

Every circumstance that favored this great enterprise was heartily welcomed. Every discovery of materials in America—of some mineral useful in the arts, some root or bark that could contribute to our pharmacopoeia—was hailed as an amendment to the Declaration of Independence. When in 1810 the first trained veterinary surgeon landed in New York, Americans expressed their gratification that

[19]

the transit of that science had begun; the naturalization of merino sheep was applauded like a victory on the battle-field. When in 1807 Joel Barlow's epic poem was published in Philadelphia, patriots deplored that it had been found necessary to make the illustrations in England, while the first volume of Alexander Wilson's handsome *Ornithology* was welcomed the following year with special satisfaction because in type, ink, paper, engraving, and binding it was American—everything except the reds and blues used in the coloring of the birds, which had to come from France. But we were not to be made free from European skill as promptly as we thought. Not long ago Mr. I. N. Phelps Stokes published his sumptuous six-volume work, *The Iconography of Manhattan Island,* which traces the physical growth of New York City, or at least its principal borough, during the three hundred years since its foundation by the Dutch. It is a striking circumstance that much of the paper and the fine engraving had to be imported from Holland. New York is, then, in some slight degree, still New Netherland.

Our emancipation has indeed been gradual, every step painfully worked out. In our texts of learning we have risen slowly from Noah Webster's spelling book, which supplanted the English Dilworth, to the latest American treatise for advanced collegiate study; our first college textbook in economics was a mere adaptation of the Scottish McCulloch; our American texts in the classics were slightly rearranged from European editions; our greatest achievement in mathematics up to 1830 was Bowditch's translation of Laplace. In 1894 Professor Florian Cajori published a general history of mathematics. The reader notices that he mentions but few Americans—none until the eighteen-seventies, the time of Benjamin Peirce. The patriotic American in his chagrin ascribes this omission to ignorance of what had been achieved on this side of the Atlantic; then he finds that the professor had four years before published a history of mathematics in the United States, a book of four hundred pages. He who well knew the contribution of America in this branch of higher learning could see, when called upon to take the broad view, how negligible it was.

In chemistry, physics, and other fields, despite the rapid strides of recent years, the story is still much the same. In the list of winners of the Nobel Prize for research in pure science America does not figure brightly. It is the office of our Department of Commerce to watch our national expenditures; in the recent heyday of prosperity Secretary Hoover pointed out that we were spending ten times as much for cosmetics as for advancing scientific knowledge. This was not true, he observed, of older civilizations. We still have much to learn from Europe; the transit of civilization to America is by no means complete.

Let us turn, however, to follow it from the Atlantic shore. To illustrate our law of transit let us look for a moment at the South. In the colonial period it was more truly a cultural province than the North, which was well advanced in the third stage when the South was in the middle of the second. The Revolution cut it off somewhat from the metropolis across the water and it became a cultural province of the North. For a long time the intellectual prestige of New England in the South was very high. The lawyers of South Carolina were very good, said Judge Ædanus Burke, but "for a Roman gladiator armed at all points, give me Pierrepont Edwards." Professor William Hooper, speaking to the University of North Carolina in 1831, cited as the ideal for southern education Bancroft and Cogswell's Round Hill School at Northampton, Massachusetts. The process of transit may be observed.

First, there were young Northerners who went South to practise their professions, like Abraham Baldwin, the Connecticut lawyer, who is called the "Father of the University of Georgia." Amos

Wheeler, a Yale graduate seeking opportunities in the same field, wrote in his diary under 1809 of a number of young friends who had gone to practise in the upland counties of that state and of two who were said to be foremost in Wilmington, North Carolina. He knew a dozen Connecticut neighbors who could advise him out of their experience— "Mr. Eben Denison . . . thinks that there are so many Yankees in Baltimore that the chance is not so good as in some parts of Virginia." The New England Society of Charleston, formed in 1819, had prominent professional men upon its rolls. There were many in later times who thus went South to teach, men like Eli Whitney, William H. Seward, William Ellery Channing, Sergeant S. Prentiss, Amos Kendall, and Jared Sparks. Even the Yankee peddler faring through the South took spelling books along with calicoes and patent gridirons.

Overlapping with this stage, the Southerners began in much greater number to send their sons to college in the North, and in the early decades of the nineteenth century from ten to thirty per cent of the attendance at Yale and Princeton was from that section. M. Moreau de Saint Méry, visiting the latter college in 1794, remarked the surprising number of young men from Virginia and the Carolinas. In the professions the tendency was even more im-

pressive; for a long time Georgia led the states outside Connecticut in attendance at the Litchfield
Law School, with South Carolina as a close com-
petitor; about half the students at the medical
school of the University of Pennsylvania were from
the South. When news of the Richmond Theatre
fire of 1811 reached Philadelphia, scores of Vir-
ginians then enrolled—one reporter said more than
a hundred—met to listen to a memorial sermon.

Meanwhile the third stage had begun. Many
collegiate institutions were established, but they
were staffed by men of Northern training. In 1804
the president of the University of Georgia was
Josiah Meigs, of Middletown, Connecticut, who
had studied at Yale and taught there; the president
of the College of South Carolina was Jonathan
Maxcy, of Attleborough, Massachusetts, who had
studied at Brown and taught there; the president
of the University of North Carolina was Joseph
Caldwell, of Lammington, New Jersey, who had
studied at Princeton and taught there. The upland
colleges were most of them heavily indebted to
Princeton. Jefferson, who contemplated importing
directly the whole faculty of the University of Ge-
neva for his institution in Charlottesville, was an exception. Up to 1830, at least, the South, as we have
said, was a cultural province of the North. Then
came the explosions that began the rift between the

sections—the abolition movement, the ominous slave rebellion, the tariff controversy, Webster's reply to Hayne; the South became painfully self-conscious, declared her cultural independence and developed a literature of her own. It will be remembered that J. P. Kennedy's *Swallow Barn,* the South's first novel of importance, appeared in 1832, Poe's first story in 1833, Simms's *Guy Rivers* in 1834, and the *Southern Literary Messenger* in 1835.

The seaboard South, when political independence was achieved, was a settled country and a fairly well-defined geographical area. But "the West" throughout American history, until recently, has been a relative term, a phenomenon of movement, a degree of settlement; what was the west of one generation was the east of the next, when the procession of the Indian, the hunter, the trader, the cattleman, the pioneer farmer, had passed by and thriving towns and cultivated countryside developed in its wake. In tracing civilization from east to west within our country we follow a transit from an organized society to one of rude beginnings, quite as obviously as in tracing the transit from Europe to America.

It is necessary first to notice, somewhat gloomily, that civilization, generally speaking, declines when it strikes the frontier. This might almost be advanced as the second law of transit. Compare the

[25]

intellectual tone of New England in the sixteen-forties with that at the end of the century, and the contrast is depressing. We may quote a passage from the autobiography of President Samuel Johnson, of King's College, writing of his student days in New England about 1714: "The condition of learning (as well as everything else) was very low in these times, indeed much lower than in the earlier time while those yet lived who had had their education in England and first settled the country. These were now gone off the stage and their sons fell greatly short of their acquirements, as through the necessity of the times they could give but little attention to the business of education." The concentrated light of local history reveals this falling off; the late Henry R. Stiles in his minute review of *Ancient Windsor,* for example, observed that the second generation did not fill the places of the fathers. The earlier leaders had been trained in Cambridge, England, the later in Cambridge, Massachusetts—and there was a difference. It is easy to forget the quiddities of the library and drawing-room when living in a forest, and even in the extreme instance to relapse into barbarism as "squaw men."

In 1840, to advance somewhat more than a century in time and less than a thousand miles in space, the percentage of illiteracy in Indiana was four-

teen; ten years later it was twenty-two. Apprecia-
tion of special training fell apace. Neither the
Indiana frontier, nor any other, developed any overpowering respect for the professional man; it must
be remembered that it was Andrew Jackson who
deprofessionalized the civil service of the country.
In 1817 the Indiana legislature, made up of men
who had come from older communities, laid down
careful rules for examination by the courts of all
candidates for the bar; in accordance with proce-
dure slowly worked out by centuries of experience,
the judges in the cases tried before them expounded
the law, leaving to the jury the decision of the facts.
But the constitution of 1851 permitted any citizen
of ordinary decency to practise law, and allowed
the jury, however ignorant, to determine what rules
of law should be applied. The legal standards for
medical practice were likewise relaxed in the frontier environment to make way for the botanical
practitioners and other short-schooled doctors. In
fact, it must be confessed that medical standards in
general declined for a time after their transit to
America.

The delicate plant can not immediately take root
in a wilderness. Men and women of refinement can
not easily become frontiersmen, as the colony of
Napoleonic exiles at Demopolis, in Alabama, sadly
illustrates. If one such could, he would soon find

that his mind was starving. The frontier can not furnish an environment of sympathy. Many Europeans later known throughout the world as great masters have in their youth contemplated a removal to America. Robert Boyle and Comenius thought seriously of following the suggestion of their friend John Winthrop, Jr., and crossing to Connecticut, but had they set up in our half-won countryside, would one have become the father of modern chemistry and the other the father of modern education? Goethe planned to come, but as an American would he have written *Faust?* Coleridge and Southey had a romantic project of starting new careers in the upper Susquehanna Valley, but had they done so in the seventeen-nineties, would they rank to-day among the great figures of literature? Whatever momentum such men might have had upon arrival, their mental energy would have spent itself without sympathy, constructive criticism, and the stimulus of competition. The frontier can not furnish support for its own distinguished minds; generally they must reach development in the metropolis. "It is certainly remarkable," observed the writer of an article on Lindley Murray in the *Literary Magazine* for January, 1804, "that the natives of America who have arrived at eminence in arts and letters have done so in a foreign country." Really it was not remarkable at all. Would Benjamin West have become a painter of world renown if he had stayed in Pennsylvania? Would Benjamin Thompson have discovered the laws of heat as a citizen of Woburn, Massachusetts? But we can not too closely limit Omnipotence; miracles may happen and genius flourish in an unpromising environment—there was Franklin, for example.

The frontier is handicapped by lack of leisure and by the migratoriness of its life, as well as its distance from the centers of culture. But while it forgets its heritage somewhat, its equalitarian standards, resulting from the homogeneity of its population, lead it to diffuse whatever it retains. It stands hopefully for mass education and therefore lays a broad, firm basis for culture as it may be imported and developed. Leisure as it comes is rather evenly distributed and Culture, written with a large C, becomes everybody's business. The woman's club of the modern type was born in the Middle West in the eighteen-fifties.

But this culture, as we have seen, is constantly modified, or, if you will, increased, by contacts with the outside world. There are constantly presented new modes from which the community may choose for imitation. The accidental carriers, the "Typhoid Marys" of ideas, are sometimes effective and sometimes not; probably the carrier's influence is most immediate when he is not much unlike the mass he touches. Indiana was mentioned, a few lines back, as a typical frontier society a hundred years ago, and perhaps the Hoosier State will serve as well as any other for our illustrations. Robert Owen's "boatload of knowledge" that pushed up the Wabash to New Harmony in 1826 was doubtless of considerable consequence to the little world of political theorists, but not much to Indiana. An elaborate history of the state has been written without mentioning the socialistic experiment which happened to take place upon its soil but which had small part in its development. It would be difficult, indeed impossible, to trace the course of the myriad unconscious carriers who were effective. Perhaps most culture, though seldom the highest, has been transmitted by such means. But many of the carriers are conscious, resolute, and constructive, yet fully sympathetic with the frontier; we may call them the civilizers. It has taken splendid courage to assume and carry through this rôle. In the early days it took physique. Could the circuit rider thrash the rowdies, the "scorners," who stood ready to break up the meeting? Could the school-teacher's digestion endure the ordeal of boarding around a neighborhood devoted to a hog-and-hominy cuisine? Could the conscientious doctor survive the forty-mile rides through the wintry forest?

But quite apart from these raw perils patent to

the sense, the civilizer always took a risk. Could he hew a way to the light through the thicket of ignorance and prejudice, as the previous pioneer had chopped his way through oak and cypress, or would he succumb and shamefully settle down to live like others in a mental shade? Was the frontier yet ready for him? There comes to mind the case of Baynard R. Hall, the first functionary in the higher education of Indiana. Indiana wanted him, but only moderately; education was not yet its ruling passion, and it paid him but two hundred dollars for a year's instruction. It was not the money that thrilled him, however, and held him to his purpose of building a state university, but the thought that he was, as he said, "the very first man since the creation of the world to read Greek in the New Purchase." It was pleasing to his vanity, no doubt, to reflect that he was the man—young professional men have often been moved to go West by the thought that they would seem more important there than at home— but I think, as a whole, the civilizers have thought as much of civilization as of themselves. The material compensation probably did not tempt them. The circuit riders got an annual payment of from fifty dollars to two hundred, and that would have been better if it had not so often been paid in "dicker," in beef, corn, butter, potatoes, leather, buckwheat flour, feathers, coon-skins, and the like.

It took courage, too, to carry to the frontier the instruments of civilization such as the printing press. This is not the tool of a man, but of a community; to sustain it the community must be literate, moderately well-to-do, and must have an economic life sufficiently organized to need an advertising medium. There was certainly a risk in taking it to the frontier. The covered wagon is familiar to us all as an epic theme, but behind it came other arks and vehicles and beasts of precious burden, freighted with as fine a hope and driven by as stout a courage, carrying, indeed, the instruments and records of the human mind. Across the screen of memory toils the Conestoga-wagon team over the Alleghenies, in 1786, to the shabby little river town at the forks of the Ohio, laden with the press, the type, the ink, the paper that were to make up John Scull's Pittsburgh *Gazette;* then from here a short year later there sets out the flatboat of John Bradford with another rude printing press and some type cut out of dogwood, which, after being jolted into sad confusion on the rough wood-way from the river down to Lexington, does full part to build the fame of that "Athens of the West"; and then in 1804, when seventeen years of effort have driven the pioneer's axe deep into the old Northwest, Elihu Stout, a printer on this paper, supported by the same faith, straps a press and type athwart pack-

[32]

horses and threads the path to far-away Vincennes. The advance of civilization by *Gazettes!*

In the pageant of the arts and sciences these humble equipages have their place, and the men who guided them. It was a desperate enterprise. Take, for example, the first newspaper in the capital of Indiana, the Indianapolis *Gazette,* printed on a clumsy Ramage press in 1822, a year after the city's foundation, in a one-room log cabin, "part of which was occupied for a family residence." The nearest post-office was sixty miles away, so that President Monroe's message delivered in the first week of December was prime news in February. The picture can be reproduced a hundred times in American history. The paper-making frontier crossed the Alleghenies not long after that of the press; it was only six years behind in Kentucky and five in the Western Reserve; but it was not till 1820 that the first type foundry was established in the Mississippi Valley. Meanwhile, books were published, especially at Cincinnati. It had taken the printing business in all its essentials thirty-five years to cross the mountains, but in the colonial period it had taken a hundred and thirty-three years to cross the sea.

Herbert Spencer's famous law was that life proceeds from homogeneity to heterogeneity, from the simple to the complex. On the frontier one can actually watch the evolution of social species. A typical Western leader in the early days was Edward Tiffin, later to be the first Governor of Ohio. He took a medical degree at the University of Pennsylvania; going to western Virginia he soon joined to that of medicine the calling of a Methodist minister; but in the letter of recommendation which he carried from President Washington to General St. Clair in charge of the Northwest Territory, he was described as one "very familiar with the law." In New England during the eighteenth century there were few clergymen, doctors, or lawyers but did some farming; certainly this was true in the early days of Indiana. Consider the case of the Reverend John M. Dickey, in Washington County in 1815, as it is reported: "Mr. Dickey . . . aided the support of his family by farming on a small scale, teaching a singing class, and writing deeds, wills, and advertisements. He also surveyed land and sometimes taught school." But this clergyman-schoolmaster-lawyer was already on the way to specialization, as apparently he did not practise medicine. Seventeenth-century ministers, even important ones like Giles Firmin and Gershom Bulkeley, had cured the body with the soul, exhibiting, as Cotton Mather said, an "Angelical conjunction." As a later example, the Reverend Samuel Seabury of North Groton and New London studied physic and practised it as a supplementary parish duty, as did his son, Samuel, who after the Revolution became the first bishop in the United States.

It would be interesting for a state historical survey to trace graphically on the map the moving frontier of the professional family doctor in its state, to see how far he was behind the thin edge of the population mass; then to see the line of first throw-off from that stem, the trained apothecary; then the line of the second branch, the dentist; then that of the third, the modern surgeon; then those of successive specialties. History is an enterprise in space as well as in time, and such maps we now recognize as an important part of its records. No one can tell what deductions might be made if such a series were set before a scholar; for the map reveals as well as illustrates. It must be remembered that it was in examining the census maps of 1890 that Professor Frederick J. Turner saw in many phases the significance of the frontier in American history.

We speak as if this march of civilization were the stuff of history alone, yet a journey from one ocean to the other would reveal how it proceeds to-day. Where is the public library frontier in 1935? The picture gallery frontier? The chamber-music frontier? What is passing into New Mexico? Montana? Arkansas? Quite obviously it is not wholly a matter of East and West. In each region throughout the country there is a center which as a provincial town, relatively speaking, receives its culture, and as a metropolis transmits it in every direction to its countryside. Each province profoundly modifies the culture it receives; each metropolis is affected by its provinces, which throw back challenges as well as contributions in the shape of their ambitious youth, who in their energy and more equalitarian standards tend to break up old stratifications—but all this is another story. It is enough here to remember that civilization is still in transit; as we move about we are all carriers in greater or less degree, and each can say with Tennyson's Ulysses, "I am a part of all that I have met."

CULTURE IN KNAPSACKS

AMONG the few old Latin maxims whose compacted truth insures a general currency even in this day of fading interest in the classics, is one which states the effect of war upon the ordinary rules of life—*Inter arma leges silent*. The social contract, one might say, is subjected to a moratorium, and all the rights of individuals so painfully defined are straightway sacrificed to the central need of the state, the need to exist. It was as the mother of tyranny that Thomas Jefferson hated war the most. But war plays havoc with duties as well as rights. Mercy, charity and even justice are leeches fastened on the will to crush the enemy and must be plucked away. The trail of war is best traced where the conflict has played back and forth across a region for a period of years, spreading fear and hate and death as it did in seventeenth-century Germany or, on a very much smaller scale, in the American Revolution—for example, in the Carolina piedmont or on the neutral ground between the upper and the lower parties in New York.

Two chaplains, one a New Englander and the other a Frenchman, who spent some time within

the southern counties of that state, have left us
their impressions. The picture drawn by Timothy
Dwight is well known : a place of cruelty and terror
where the confidence in mankind upon which society must rest had been burned away. The testi-
mony of the Abbé Robin is not less striking:

As we approach New York, between the lines of both
armies, we see more and more of the sorrowful vestiges
of war and desolation—the houses plundered, ruined,
abandoned or burnt. These Americans so soft, pacific
and benevolent by nature, are here transformed into
monsters implacable, bloody and ravenous; party rage
has kindled a spirit of hatred between them; they attack
and rob each other by turns, destroy dwelling houses, or
establish themselves therein by driving out those who
had before dispossessed others. War, that terrible
scourge to arts and populations, is still more so to the
morals of a people, because a change in these for the
worse is the more difficult to repair.

It was not to be expected that the higher learning,
a tender shoot at best on this untamed continent,
should prosper under the tread of armies. For seven
years it was cut off from its customary nourishment
that had come from contact with the culture stores
of Great Britain. The saved-up surplus of America
itself, which in normal times might have been devoted to its endowment and equipment, was now

for the most part captured for defense. Among the clergy in the North, Tory scholars of Anglican faith like President Myles Cooper were soon lost to American learning, while in the Whig party there were those like President Witherspoon quite as ruthlessly deflected from the steady edification of the classroom to set their talents to the work of war committees.

When in 1775 argument with England gave place to armed resistance, there were nine institutions in America which deserved the name of college. Not one of these could continue its full routine of academic exercise without interruption throughout the period. Learning was the first thing to be sacrificed. Seven of the nine, all but Yale and Dartmouth, were occupied as hospitals, barracks or stables by armed forces; three of them, Harvard, New Jersey and King's College, to greater or less degree, by both armies in succession. The succession was rapid indeed at Princeton where Nassau Hall changed hands three times within a single day. In most cases books and philosophical apparatus were moved away for storage in obscurity; usually they did not return intact, most of such property belonging to King's College, for example, being destroyed or lost forever. During the seven years of occupation there was virtually no teaching under the authority of that institution, and Brown and Pennsylvania, to give them their modern names, did little better. Queen's College was scattered from New Brunswick when Hessian soldiers took possession of its campus, and it maintained so precarious a course throughout the war, now in an old abandoned log church, now in a distant farm house, that it scarcely lived at all from 1776 to 1781. At Princeton the floors were broken up for firewood, and other damage wreaked upon the building, so that after the trustees regained possession some five years were required to put it into shape. The halls at Providence were scarcely better when the French took out their invalids and horses in the spring of 1782. Invested funds for higher education were likewise ill-maintained. Princeton, for example, lost £10,000 of her endowment and Dartmouth suffered heavily because it could not realize upon the promises which had been made in England.

But the records of the mind are not found exclusively within such academic walls. As we call up the picture of scarlet-coated wreckers tearing down the Old North Meetinghouse in Boston to feed their winter fires, we remember that these eight years of war destroyed many an architectural monument, of humble place, perhaps, in the huge catalog of human art, but among the best the American communities possessed. For the riding school into which these unwelcome visitors turned the neigh-

boring Old South, such fuel was not enough, and
they filled their stove with rare books and manu-
scripts from Thomas Prince's library, cutting off
forever from posterity's ken some episodes of
Massachusetts' early history. The largest collection
of books then existing in North America, with its
nearly seven thousand volumes, the Charleston Library, was consumed in the fire of January, 1778,
supposed to have been set by British incendiaries.
There were cultural losses, too, in the other great
fires incident to the war: those at Falmouth,
Charlestown, New York and Norfolk, besides
those towns wasted at the hands of Benedict Arnold
and William Tryon. In decorative art the torch is
recognized as the symbol of civilization; it was
not so remembered by the citizens of Danbury,
Fairfield and Norwalk, and of New London and
Richmond.

Private collections were despoiled, paintings
wantonly destroyed. On the stately portrait of Cad-
wallader Colden by Matthew Pratt, now hanging
in the Great Hall of the Chamber of Commerce in
New York, still may be seen the scars made by the
British grenadiers, tossing it back and forth upon
their bayonets in the street, till a passer-by informed
them that the original was not a rebel merchant but
His Majesty's late Lieutenant Governor; how
many canvases throughout the country went unres-

cued the record cannot show. The German mercenaries were especially notorious—Von Heister, "the arch plunderer," was long remembered—taking toll of Tory as well as Whig, carrying off the plate and treasures from Colonel William Axtell's country seat at Flatbush, taking everything of value from the mansion of Daniel Coxe at Trenton, rifling and sacking in particular the homes of the rich who lived well, whose furnishings, as might have been expected, most reflected thought and taste. The American soldier likewise stood in no awe of art.

Paintings disappeared, like Smibert's portrait of Dr. Caner of old King's Chapel; fine furniture was scattered and destroyed, like that of Colonel John Stuart in South Carolina; family plate, however beautifully fashioned, came to a like end, such as that which the Earl of Loudoun had presented to Hugh Wallace, the provincial councillor of New York. The melting pot was always waiting. As a single example of what happened in many homes, take the case of the Reverend John Sayre, rector of Fairfield, Connecticut, and persecuted by both sides. He lost a "large and genteel library of the best authors in physic, history, divinity and philosophy," about six hundred volumes; "four family pictures done to the life by Mr. West, elegantly framed, cost £70 Philadelphia per pair"; "eight pieces of painting done on oak" and "fancy pictures neatly framed and glazed"; also busts, furniture, jewelry and, most precious of all, the consecrated vessels of his church.

It would be wearisome to bring forth further illustrations of the losses in learning and the arts which America sustained by reason of the war. We need not here conjecture whether or not the war was necessary to make a great America possible; probably independence would not otherwise have been achieved; if so, the benefit was worth the cost. We are concerned with the process of war itself and its effect upon the culture of the country. In general war is an enterprise of destruction and any gains to culture from its actual administration are quite incidental. Nevertheless, some gains were registered.

The contacts at the council board or on the tented field by which the canny Yankees and the spirited Southern planters came to know and respect each other, made America more nearly a community than it otherwise would have been for many a year. As one fingers over the letters of John Adams from Philadelphia, New York and other places, one realizes that they are the record of a personal education. Adams soon came to realize the truth in Joseph Hawley's counsel to the Massachusetts delegates to Congress when he told them that they would doubtless meet there gentlemen "fully equal to yourselves or any of you, in their knowledge of

Great Britain, the colonies, law, history, government, commerce, etc." Sojourning in New York between campaigns, a group of New Englanders enjoyed the unaccustomed privilege of instruction in the dance by the well-known master Mr. Trotter. So tutored, observed Dr. Thacher in his *Journal,* they hoped eventually to cut a "figure in the ballroom." Travel in itself was broadening, and Carolina rangers may have refined their taste during their sojourn in the Pennsylvania capital in 1778–1779; Dutch farmer lads from the Hudson Valley doubtless learned a little of the world on the long march down to Yorktown.

Business organization was immensely stimulated by the military need. It is an unpleasant picture that an historian draws of sleek speculators at their desks in comfortable Boston counting-houses casting up their profits of one or two hundred per cent on woolen goods, while soldiers shivered and died at Valley Forge. But doubtless most of the activity was legitimate and valuable; certainly it advanced the technique as well as the volume of domestic commerce in this country. Manufactures, which had been inappropriate in provinces in touch with the settled industries of the metropolis across the sea, now sprouted hopefully in many a household and by many a stream, especially in articles of outfit for the troops—ammunition, iron, cloth and leather.

The metal mills of Springfield and Worcester, for instance, whose inland situation made them safe from the British, date from the Revolution. "Historical events," remarks an anthropologist, "appear to have been more potent in leading races to civilization than their faculty." Avoiding the old controversy that peeks out from this theorem, it may safely be maintained that social function is diversified and improved when we are shaken out of our routine of custom, that progress is accelerated by successive crises, that thought comes out of need—all of which is a fine academic way of saying that "Necessity is the mother of invention." In this consideration war refunds a little of what it robs from civilization.

If abstract science is deserted, that which can be instantly applied to building or conserving fighting strength enjoys the most assiduous cultivation. Medicine is an obvious example. Many doctors—one historian risks the figure of four thousand—served their country in the eight years of the Revolution and learned much from the service. Most of them had never had an opportunity before to go inside a hospital or to come into contact with a real master of their profession. The first American book on medicine appeared for their instruction—Professor John Jones's *Plain, Concise, Practical Remarks on the Treatment of Wounds and Frac-*

tures (N. Y., October, 1775)—and a creditable beginning it was. Under like stimulus appeared the first pharmacopœia to be printed in this country, a thirty-two page pamphlet by one of the physicians-general, Dr. William Brown. Such doctors as Morgan, Shippen and Rush, in their conspicuous service won a prestige which made their beneficent leadership far more effective than it otherwise could have been in the time of peace to come. Probably most historians will agree with a scholarly soldier-surgeon that, "The War of Independence was the making of medicine in this country."

The incidental gains so far considered were of domestic origin. In speaking of the losses, account was taken of the fact that we were deprived for seven years of the normal culture importation so needed in a young and growing country. But there was some offset to this loss by reason of the sojourn of the three European armies, not only the French, who came to help the Whigs, but also, though in smaller degree, from the forces, the British and the German, who came to vindicate the Tories.

About one hundred and fifty thousand Europeans landed at our ports in uniform, one hundred and ten thousand of them British, thirty thousand Germans, and somewhat less than six thousand French, but if there be added those who manned the two foreign fleets and who were ashore from time to time, the total was much larger. Also there must be counted in the soldiers of fortune and the gentlemen volunteers from many countries. They were, of course, professional armies; especially was this true of the Germans from Hesse-Cassel, Hesse-Hanau, Brunswick, Anspach-Bayreuth, Waldeck and Anhalt-Zerbst, who like the old condottieri or certain regiments of Swiss and Scotch, had long fought for pay; none of the three European forces were national armies in the modern sense. They afford, then, a fair illustration of such phenomena in general. It will be interesting to study how armies carry culture, as it were, in their knapsacks.

It scarcely needs be said that carrying culture was not their major purpose. They were not like the Mohammedan hordes who at the sword's point forced invaded peoples to accept their view of life, nor like the armies sent forth by Carnot and Bonaparte who were told by their commanders that they carried with them the blessings of liberty, fraternity and equality. In a sense the British came to teach us the merit of obeying one's king, but it is not likely that they looked upon it as a crusade or thought that they were sowing ideas on a waiting soil. Even less probable is it that private soldiers in any of the three armies worried much about themselves as carriers of culture or had a very high degree of it to carry. Historically the private soldier, even when not fighting, has spread more wretchedness than benefit in the districts he has invaded. An early eighteenth-century writer, Edward Ward, who knew him well, says in his saucy essay on *Mars Stript of his Armour* (1709) that his main concerns are victuals and drink: "If he ever thinks at all (and truly that's a Question), it is of being a Captain; and then he pleases himself with the Fancy of how he'll maul the Men and the Women." In these armies of the old régime it is the officers, quite naturally, to whom we must look for ideas, graces or special competences which might be communicated.

We must notice in the first place a certain cultural gain when armies fight side by side as allies. Each learns the good points of the other, and generally there results a mutual respect if not affection, which, as far as it goes, is valuable. It was thus, possibly, that internationalism began in the Crusades. This new confidence is not suddenly and easily achieved, as memories not more than fifteen or twenty years old may testify to-day. In 1776 the mercenaries did not like the food the English ship-cooks furnished them and they resented "the proud insulting look which the English are wont to cast at the Germans"; but afterward they seem to have got on very well. The problem was more serious in the case of the Americans and the French. Here not only were two nations coöperating for the first time, but they had behind them a long tradition of mistrust and, indeed, of hatred. Three generations of Americans, especially the Yankees on the north frontier, carrying through four wars, had been taught to shudder at the name of Frenchman—"the French," wrote the Reverend Samuel Niles, shortly after 1760, "our cruel, designing, fierce enemies."

If laws are silent in the clash of arms, the critical instinct is sound asleep. Credulity as to the enemy's devilish ingenuity is matched only by the certainty that God is fighting on "our side." When in 1711 Hovenden Walker's fleet was turned back by the storm in the Gulf of St. Lawrence, the pious Mother Juchereau had written: "The least devout were touched by the grandeur of the miracle wrought in our behalf—a marvelous effect of God's love for Canada, which of all these countries, is the only one which professes the true religion." On the other hand, when, thirty-five years later, a storm played similar havoc with the Duke d'Anville's ninety-seven sail, daily expected to overwhelm the port of Boston, the Reverend Thomas Prince could mount the pulpit, as Longfellow plausibly pictures him, to offer up his Protestant prayer for God's deliverance: .

> And even as I prayed
> The answering trumpet came. . . .
> O Lord! before thy path
> They vanished and ceased to be,
> When thou didst walk in wrath
> With thine horses through the sea.

Religious prejudice had constantly embittered the contact in the North, but the feeling was not confined to that region. Washington had fought the French and he characterized them as "a crafty, savage enemy . . . , barbarians, for they deserve no better name."

If such was the old opinion as to the fundamental character of the French, reading and report had produced as vivid a misconception of their manners and appearance. Many had read the *Spectator,* wherein they were presented as a "ludicrous nation," their women "fantastical" and their men "vain and lively." The Abbé Robin gathered that the Americans had pictured Frenchmen as "busy frizzing their hair and painting their faces, without faith or morals." It will not surprise us who have been familiar with war hates not so long ago to find that enemies may be conceived as pampered

dandies at the same time that they are thought barbarians. Some doubted the desirability of an alli-
ance with such a people. It was true that a man
named Montesquieu had written very sanely about
politics, but as for a considerable element among
the French having any notion of free government,
the idea was ridiculous. Samuel Adams asked the
brilliant secretary of Steuben where he had learned
republican principles. "In France," replied young
Duponçeau. "In France!" exclaimed the Man of
the Town Meeting, "that is impossible." Then re-
covering himself in a hearty effort to be courteous,
he added, "Well, because a man was born in a
stable, it is no reason why he should be a horse."

It was a general notion that the "mounseers"
were diminutive, spindle-shanked and cadaverous.
When the Count d'Estaing's fleet reached Boston,
the curious populace were amazed to see plump
and portly officers and strong, vigorous sailors.
There was some trick here! The wily French had
picked out the best specimens they could find and
put them into the first boats so as to make a handsome impression! But boatload after boatload bore
in upon the Yankee's understanding the astonishing
fact that Frenchmen looked like other people.
"Neither the officers nor the men," wrote William
Channing to Ezra Stiles somewhat later, "are the
effeminate beings we were heretofore taught to be-

lieve them. They are as large and likely men as can be produced by any nation." Thus unlearning ancient prejudice the New England heart began to open, but it took some time for old conventional conceptions to dissolve in its expanding warmth. There was the matter of food, for instance; the French were reported to have preposterous tastes. An attempt of American hospitality to meet this situation must be told in full.

Nathaniel Tracy, who lived in a large house in Cambridge, prepared a feast for the French admiral, the consul and the officers:

Tracy filled a plate of soup which went to the admiral, and the next was handed to the consul. As soon as L'Etombe [the consul] put his spoon into the plate he fished up a large frog, just as green and perfect as if he had hopped from the pond into the tureen. . . . As soon as he had throughly inspected it and made himself sure of the matter, he exclaimed "Ah! Mon Dieu! un grenouille!" . . . The company, convulsed with laughter, examined the soup plates as the servants brought them, and in each was to be found a frog. The uproar was universal. Meantime Tracy kept his ladle going, wondering what his outlandish guests meant by their extravagant merriment. "What's the matter?" asked he, and raising his head surveyed the frogs dangling by a leg in all directions. "Why don't you eat them?" he exclaimed. "If they knew the confounded trouble I had to catch them in order to treat them to a dish of their own country, they would find that with me, at least, it was no joking matter."

The reasonableness of the French diet occasioned surprise everywhere. The French, wrote Colonel Fontaine of the Virginia militia, "are very different from the ideas formerly inculcated in us of a people living on frogs and coarse vegetables."

France sent an extraordinary military force, small in numbers though it was. Walking back a few miles from the east bank of the Hudson and looking out across the hills of Westchester with the eye of imagination, one may people them again with the proud troops who camped there a hundred and fifty years ago—the Deux-Ponts in sky-blue skirted coats and white small clothes, the Saintonge in white and green, the Bourbonnais in white piped with black and the Soissonnais, most picturesque of all, with rose-colored facings and plumes. The officers, with hardly an exception, were chosen from the old noblesse of France. There were princes, marquises, dukes, counts, barons, chevaliers, heirs to the polish of their ancient stock. For instance, there were the Prince de Broglie, the Count de Custine and that shameless rake and gallant commander, the Duke de Lauzun, all to suffer death as aristocrats a dozen years later on the Paris scaffold. There was the Marquis de Bouillé who in 1791 was to arrange the flight of Louis of France and his restless queen to Varennes; there was the Count de Fersen, who was to drive their carriage on the first stage of that fatal ride; and there, too, Count Dumas, who as agent of the Assembly was to escort them on their ignominious return. There were young men of power who were to be men of eminence, like Count Berthier, who as Prince of Wagram was to be Napoleon's chief of staff, and, on the other hand, Count de Saint-Simon, who was to be the first great socialist of the coming century. There were scholars, also, the Marquis de Chastellux, the youngest academician of France, and the Count de Ségur, the historian, who was likewise to find a place among the Immortals. These ten may give a sample of the quality of the officers who served under Rochambeau.

On the whole they and their men behaved with exemplary circumspection, adapting themselves to the habits and conditions of America. It was with much truth that La Luzerne, the French minister at Philadelphia, could write the French commander near the end of 1782, "Your well-behaved and brave army has . . . destroyed in three years prejudices deep-rooted for three centuries." America emerged from the war acquainted and pleased with the French, in itself a cultural gain. Teachers of

the language increased in number and the book-
stores added stocks of French books. Fine ladies
talked of French styles and hoped that they might
have them more promptly in the future than in the
past, when they had had to wait for slow transmis-
sion through the London imitations. The excesses
of the Revolution made sympathy with France a
party question, but French cultural influence was
never lost. Much of all this was the long result of
the excellent quality and behavior of the French
army in America.

Obviously one way in which armies influence
the culture of regions they invade is by remaining
there as colonists. The invasions of the Visigoths,
the Ostrogoths, the Vandals, were merely migra-
tions fighting their way. The armies of 1775–1780
were not so moved, and yet in the reckoning this
item must be counted. We know, for example, that
many soldiers of the British army thus took an in-
expensive voyage—possibly they were Scotchmen
—with such permanent residence in view. There
was doubtless many a farmer who so helped to tame
the wilderness and many an artisan who added his
skill to the resources of America, like the carriage-
maker whom "Peter Parley" could recall as staying
in Connecticut and fashioning the first chaise in
the town of Ridgefield. Otherwise what became of
the thousands who informally renounced allegiance

to King George by the simple process of desertion?

The largest proportion of permanent colonists was from the Germans. Of the thirty thousand who came, twelve thousand five hundred never returned. American marksmanship accounts for these in many cases, but probably a large part stayed to grow up with the country. At the close of the war pamphlets were published in German by South Carolina, New Jersey and Nova Scotia inviting the mercenaries to remain and take up land at bargain prices. There was little inducement for some of them to cross the sea again. Seven years had brought not a few to an age when retirement from the army would be welcome if not necessary. The Duke of Brunswick, realist that he was, foresaw that so large an old-soldier element would not make for peace in his domain and issued a proclamation virtually forbidding many to come home; return passage would be paid only for native Brunswickers in good health. At least twenty-eight Brunswick officers remained and many troops. Of the eleven hundred German prisoners brought to Reading, Pennsylvania, in 1782, only about three hundred went back to Germany. Those who stayed settled as individuals here and there, the largest group in Baltimore. Their skill in handicrafts was praised as notable and all observers of their prison camps paid tribute to their gardens, which attracted visitors from considerable distances.

The armies of the old régime, as has been indicated, were officered almost always from the gentry, when not from the nobility. That their presence in a province affected the deportment of its citizens had been noticed long before. Doubtless, as the clergy charged, they brought a complement of fashionable vices; doubtless too, as many a *Charlotte Temple* soon discovered, their polished manners did not always mean a fine regard for other people's lasting happiness. But, at any rate, by their example they contributed some grace to social intercourse. The succession of British majors and captains who in the seventeen-sixties lodged with the mother of Alexander Graydon certainly affected the young life of that interesting memoirist. It was under their encouragement, apparently, that he learned dancing, French and the invaluable art of repartee.

In the Revolution, polite society in Philadelphia, or at least the Tory part of it, had never had such a winter as when Howe's army occupied the city. The *Mischianza,* with its Knights of the Blended Rose and of the Burning Mountain and their lovely damsels, was only the climax of a season full of brilliant routs and dinners. A modish young lady, wrote Rebecca Franks, might rake (the word is hers) as much as she pleased. But the Whigs, in their towns, had even better opportunities than the Tories; they had more polished instructors in the courtly officers from France. True there was some difficulty in the matter of language; however, language is but one form of expression or communication. The Count de Ségur writes of balls in 1782, to which people flocked for ten leagues around and where local merchants' daughters danced with nobles lately from Versailles. They must have made some headway toward reforming the stiffly ordered dancing parties formerly the custom, of which De Chastellux so vehemently complained. At any rate, French dancing masters were more in demand after the war than before.

A more marked effect of European armies in this country was the introduction of the code of honor. Duels were infrequent in colonial days and when they took place a military man was generally involved; during the French and Indian War, while the British officers were here, precedents were set that were followed much more commonly when the greater war began. The coming of the French gave the code still higher standing. Lafayette represented the chivalry of his caste, though with some extravagance, when he wanted to settle the war by challenging to single combat the Earl of Carlisle, whom the English ministry had sent over as a peace commissioner. Young America came to believe that, in the phrase of Dr. Jameson, "if greatly displeased with the conduct of a fellow-citizen toward you, your proper course was to offer him an opportunity to kill you." "You may judge," wrote Janet Montgomery to Sarah Jay in September, 1780, "how fashionable duelling has grown, when we have had five in one week." This most obvious effect upon our manners was without a doubt deplorable, but probably as a whole the social influence of the European officers was fortunate.

The armies likewise made some contribution to the arts, especially the social arts of entertainment. Forced back upon themselves for their diversion, the officers at garrison posts have oftentimes resorted to the stage. Mrs. Anne Grant tells us that she saw the British soldiers act before the colonials in Albany. At the end of the century it was an American garrison which introduced the drama to Detroit and, relying solely on themselves, maintained it quite creditably for a quarter of a century, largely in an old brick storehouse at the foot of Wayne Street equipped with home-made scenery. Later still, marching with the guardians of the frontier, the muses of the drama raised their temple at Fort Snelling. For example, in 1836 we find the soldiers enacting *Monsieur Tonson* and *The Vil-*

lage Barber to great applause, the lovely heroine Adolphine de Courey captivating her Jack Ardourly, both probably having spent the morning cleaning guns or drilling an awkward squad.

Soldier drama likewise whiled away the tedium of barracks life during the Revolutionary War, especially among the British officers. They introduced the theatre as an institution into Boston, though, as has been remarked, they may have produced plays there not so much to amuse themselves as to affront the Puritans. In his prologue for their production of the tragedy of *Zara,* General Burgoyne recalled the troubles of the drama in Cromwell's time and then observes:

> To sooth the times too much resembling these,
> And lull the care-tir'd thought, this stage arose.
> Proud if you hear, rewarded if you're pleased,
> We come to minister to minds diseased.

Probably not many of the "minds diseased" were present to profit by these ministrations; most native critics would scarcely approve the tone of such pieces as the general's farce entitled *The Blockade of Boston.* Nevertheless, it was something to give that pious capital its first season of the drama.

Wherever the British soldiers stayed for any length of time the stage appeared. When in their Virginia prison camp, they put up a "Comedy

House," which neighboring Americans for a time attended, a harlequin painted on the curtain pointed to these words: "Who would have expected us here?" There was a lively season of the soldier drama in Philadelphia, and the scenery which Major André painted was afterward in more or less continuous use there until the theatre burned in 1821. In 1780, after the British had left, the first French play in America, Beaumarchais's *Eugenie,* was presented there under the ægis of the French army, Congress's law against stage plays having been lifted in its favor. In New York the drama flourished for half a dozen years continuously, under British military auspices, rising from eighteen performances in 1777 to thirty-five in 1781. *The Rivals* and *The School for Scandal,* among other plays, were thus given their New York *premières,* and the performances in the "Theatre Royal" in John Street were accounted very good. Unlike such productions elsewhere, the female parts were taken by real women—"such as followed the drum." Of course, the stage was no novelty in New York, but its continuance there when professional actors had left the country affected the taste of the considerable population who lived within the lines. A local generation passed from childhood to maturity under its influence. One night in the spring of 1777 a boy in wide-eyed wonder saw the soldiers enact *The Beaux Stratagem*. Fascinated by the romantic illusion of his first play, the little William Dunlap could never afterward escape it; it was thus that he became the Father of American Drama.

Other arts were fostered in America by the officers, especially those who stayed. One has but to mention Major L'Enfant to recall that we owe to a French military man much of the beauty of our national capital. It was he, too, who designed the badge of the Society of the Cincinnati and thus fixed for good the eagle as the symbol of America. What other architects remained would be hard to say, but probably William Spratt, who built the charming Deming place in Litchfield and other houses in Connecticut, was not the only British officer who decided to invest his talent in this growing country. Music, too, received some impulse. As the fife had been introduced by the British forces in the French and Indian War, so now they and the Germans brought the brass band to America, a balanced instrumentation having been developed in Europe which was hitherto unknown in our provincial capitals. The excellent concerts on Boston Common were one form of British activity to which the Puritan "minds diseased" took no exception; the most notable performances were in Trinity Churchyard in New York, though their presence there was thought a little inappropriate by some citizens and the outraged Hannah Lawrence exclaimed:

> Heavens! shall a mean inglorious train
> The mansions of our dead profane?

On the whole there were more and better musicians with the armies than had visited America before.

Armies sometimes affect the religious thought of those with whom they come in contact, as is plentifully illustrated in the history of the Roman Empire. In the last French war, this phenomenon had been remarked. The Reverend Ezra Stiles writing in 1759 was disheartened at the influence of British officers: ". . . I judge the American Morals & Religion were never in so much danger as from our Concern with the Europeans in the present war. . . . I look upon it that our Officers are in Danger of being corrupted with vicious principles, & many of them I doubt not will in the End of the War come home minute philosophers initiated in the polite Mysteries & vitiated morals of Deism." According to Timothy Dwight such prophecies were sadly realized and the New England clergy were hard put to it to counteract the influence of British infidel officers; then, he says, there came a second wave by reason of the French. Samuel Hopkins thought that infinite damage had been done to faith in Newport by the presence of the allied troops. Yet as far as the French were concerned these reverend gentlemen may have read their fears more clearly than the facts. It would have been difficult for American officers to understand French infidelity; and the large majority of the French who came were not infidels.

As for the religious influence of the armies in the Revolution, probably the most important was the public celebration of the mass in many communities for the first time. Ninety chaplains came here with the French ships; and Catholicism first appeared, outside of Maryland, under really friendly auspices. Some remained to labor in the new country; there was the Abbé Poterie, for example, who was the founder of the church in Boston. Others officiated at improvised altars in American towns, baptized children and revived the piety of Catholics long removed from priestly ministrations. It was a "singular and affecting" sight, as good Dr. Thacher says, to see the Congress of the United States, the Assembly and Council of Pennsylvania and "a number of principal gentlemen of the various orders" gathered in the Catholic Church in Philadelphia to listen to the Abbé Bandol preach a sermon on the late glorious success of the allied armies; then the legislators, most of them doubtless for the first time, heard the Latin *Te Deum* sung.

After the French had gone the Catholic church might still seem an exotic, but at least it was known by sight.

In science, no less than in religion and the arts, the sojourn of European troops was instructive to America, but largely science in its useful application. Washington said that he had but one native engineer in whom he could place confidence; Duportail, Launoy, Radière, Gouvion, L'Enfant and Queneret brought invaluable technique, some of them staying after the war and illustrating their science in public works. So far as the civil application was an outgrowth of the military, American engineering may be said to date from the arrival of these French officers.

Armies, as has been observed, have need of competent surgical aid and it might well be expected that expeditionary forces would bring gentlemen of that faculty whose presence in the new country would be helpful. After the French and Indian war a number of British army surgeons stayed to practice in our larger towns and did much to raise the tone of the profession. During the Revolution James Thacher and others had opportunity to witness and admire the skill of such Englishmen in the hospital at Albany after Burgoyne's surrender. He was struck with their celerity, and in those preanæsthetic days, when every second might seem a very age of agony, celerity was paramount. Americans learned not a little from the example of the British military administration in dietetics. Elbridge Gerry, speaking of the enemy's use of vinegar and vegetables in soldiers' rations warmly recommended imitation in the American diet. When the French fleet came to Boston, young John Warren, who later founded the Harvard Medical School, cultivated the society of the doctors, acquiring all the knowledge he could. "Thus," says his son, "though he had not been to Europe, Europe may be said to have come to him." The French medical men gave no formal instruction, but their influence was felt. Dr. Benjamin Rush in writing his paper upon tetanus drew much from his observation of French military surgeons. Before the army left in 1782 the scholarly medical director Jean François Coste delivered at William and Mary College his famous oration entitled *De Antiqua Medico-Philosophia Orbi Novo Adaptanda.*

Of all American professionals none to-day enjoy a higher reputation throughout the world than the dentists. It is interesting to note that before the Revolution such practitioners in America were few, scattered and meagerly equipped—English itinerants, being skilful barber-surgeons or physicians with a side-line. Now it happened that the French navy required its surgeons to know as much as could be learned as to the scientific treatment of the teeth, though naturally some mastered more of that branch than their colleagues. During the idle months of 1781 while the allied forces were encamped at Providence, Dr. James Gardette and Dr. Joseph Le Maire not only eased the pain in many a Gallic jaw, but also demonstrated the science to American visitors from far and near. These two decided to remain and practice in America, but that is not what makes them most significant. During that season at Providence they systematically taught their specialty to an ambitious Yankee lad, Josiah Flagg, and qualifying thus the first American dentist, as by an apostolic laying on of hands, may be credited with transferring to America a science which was to flourish so eminently upon its soil.

The historian is rarely able to take censuses. He employs statistics eagerly enough when contemporaries have left them all compiled, but in the history of society, at least, he usually must make his arduous inductions upon such samples as he can find. He must humbly realize the fewness of his facts and not crush them with too vast an edifice of inference. But the instances we have brought forward will surely warrant us in concluding that the transit of civilization to America was not wholly halted by a long and engrossing war with a European power and that the seeds of culture may be

[67]

carried where one might not look to find them, in the knapsacks of the soldiers.

That soldiers carry *home* ideas and tastes was abundantly proved in the Crusades, when the northern Christians went to crush Mohammedans and returned to advertise Mohammedan wares. Charles VIII's return with his army from Italy in 1495 is said really to have brought the Renaissance to France. Armies will bring back unexpected things. Courtesy, that prime constituent of medieval chivalry, is said to have been derived from contact with the paynims in the wars of Charlemagne; to take a very different example, no one had thought that Norwegian soldiers imprisoned in England during the Napoleonic wars would be the means of introducing Quakerism into Norway. It is worth inquiring whether the European soldier took back ideas when peace had been concluded, though it must be borne in mind that they could scarcely learn much of the arts of civilization in America, for they knew a higher development at home; nations and individuals could oftentimes learn many things from cultural inferiors, but they seldom do.

Yet the broadening influence of travel was felt, and even the trivial little surprises that were bound to come had some slight value in making minds a bit more objective. The French were interested to see men shaking hands; they remarked that American ladies occasionally washed their hair, and other odd customs. The Hessians found the New England town a queer political phenomenon, neither seigniory nor city—apparently a little province; searching the landscape with their soldiers' eyes, they at first thought that our common rail fences had been erected as impediments to cavalry. It interests us to note that they found the cost of living high in America and that American women dressed beyond their station. Certainly they learned respect for the Americans—"I pray you," wrote home De Loos, "to give up the Hessian notion that the Rebels are not brave"—and they were astonished at the general prosperity they observed among the Dutch in the southern counties of New York: "The inhabited parts . . ." wrote Henkelmann, "are built up with the most beautiful houses, situated on the most agreeable sites. Their furniture would satisfy the finest tastes, and is of a quality that we cannot boast of at home. At the same time everything is so clean and shining that I can hardly describe it." They were astonished to see John Hancock, the President of Congress, going to market with a basket, but this last strange spectacle and all that it represented was what most charmed the French.

Many French officers had read about liberty and they came expecting to find it and to fight for it.

As two French historians, M. Jusserand and Professor Faÿ have recently contended, it was for them a war of enthusiasm rather than a war of calculation; the young liberal nobles had belabored old Maurepas into war for love of liberalism and not for hatred of England. They found more than they had hoped. From a highly mannered and sophisticated society they stepped into one of striking simplicity; it had for them the luxury of a rest cure, with all the virtues that philosophy had dreamed. The Count de Ségur marvelled at the decorum of Americans "and the order and wise liberty which characterized the New Republic, where happiness was so firmly established from the cradle." De Chastellux applauded their toleration in religion and their purity of morals. "Licentious manners," he says, "are so foreign to America, that the communication with young women leads to nothing bad." They were delighted with the simple dignity of Americans which they interpreted as rising from the general sense of equality in status.

American constitutionalism and American equality—this was the lesson the French army carried home; and to put it into our figure, they carried seeds whose explosive force was to shake the very ground of France. The liberal left of the Constituent Assembly in 1789 included most of the young nobles who had served in America; Count Alexandre Lameth, in the "triumvirate," had been an aide to Rochambeau; Lafayette was one of the most prominent men in the Assembly. It will be remembered that the end of the feudal régime was precipitated on August fourth by the fine frenzy of the Viscount de Noailles, a veteran of Yorktown. Certainly the officers who had served in the expeditionary force of 1780 did their part to make America the ideal of the French Revolution, at least in its earlier phases.

Bearing in mind the lessons learned in politics and sociology, we may inquire as to whether these military visitors, and through them the world, learned anything of science. They certainly brought no scientific corps as did Alexander when, not content with the homage of conquered peoples, he sought the sources of the great streams of their countries, from the Nile to the Indus—not every commander had had Aristotle as a tutor—or Napoleon who, while striking at the Mamelukes and British, set his savants to read the mysteries of Egypt. As has been said, the armies were not likely to learn much of art or technology in America, but as a great unexploited field of nature, America would present to the scholarly officer, if such there were, a boundless range of effort.

Under this stimulus few, if any, productions came from British pens. The French did but little better; De Chastellux saw the opportunity but neither he nor his colleagues embraced it. True enough, some like Closen made casual collections of stuffed animals; the Abbé Robin examined the stones in all the churchyards from Boston to Williamsburg, so he says, to note the average life expectancy, but one doubts the soundness of his science when, in conclusion, he supports De Pauw's old thesis that all life grows feeble in the New World! The French and the British came and went without adding any valuable work to the literature of science.

By tradition we remember the German mercenaries as stupid men led by stupid men; and yet tradition may succumb to a surprise attack such as we are trying here. German mental habits may have had their own peculiar character, but they were happily adapted to the task of systematic observation. "A cold German," says a writer in the *Gentleman's Magazine* for December, 1788, "a cold German, whose erudition is boundless, who collects the most minute facts, and who has not even fancy enough to form one conjecture, is worth thousands of ingenious dabblers, whose light is a mere *ignis fatuus* and only dazzles to mislead." When it came to solid, accurate accumulation, observed another article, the Germans were the best reliance. "Germany is the land of erudition, the

Northern kingdoms of national history and antiquities, Spain of superstition, Italy of poetry, England of natural philosophy and mathematics, and France of every science," but reaching most distinction in *belles lettres*. Against the background of this general judgment, let us glance at the mercenary forces of 1776 and 1777.

There are hints of scientific curiosity even in the diaries of the transport voyages, such as the minute examination of an octopus, or a comparative study by laboratory methods of the saltiness of the water in different sections of the sea. Lieutenant Hinrichs, who conducted the latter, had joined this military expedition, it seems, largely because of its opportunities for scientific observation. But the first distinguished name is that of Johann David Schoepf, who came at the age of twenty-five as chief surgeon with the Anspach-Bayreuth troops. Trained at the University of Erlangen in medicine and natural science, he already had a reputation as an authority on mines. Insatiably curious as to nature in America, he found his casual notes taken during the war were insufficient and remained a year and a half for further study. His *Travels* published a few years later, present a vivid picture of society, but are most valuable upon the aspect of the country. On the basis of his American observations he contributed an extraordinary list of scientific works. He published what is commonly regarded the first systematic work on American geology; he noted the relative uniformity of the coastal plain, saw that it was emerging in the South, and first marked out the "fall line." He wrote the first paper on American ichthyology, the first on American frogs, the first on American turtles. He described American diseases, made the first attempt at a full American *Materia Medica* and before the war was over published a scientific account of the American climate, unsurpassed for many years. Surely this many-sided contribution entitles Dr. Schoepf to a place in the history of science in America, whatever uniform he wore.

One of the subjects on which Schoepf had taken notes, but never published, was the American forest, where he says he felt bound to defer to a fellow officer of special competence. Frederick Adam Julius, Baron von Wangenheim, a captain in the Hessian jäger corps, published in 1781 his *Beschreibung einiger Nordamerikanischer Holz- und Buscharten . . . ,* which though issued at Göttingen, was dated at Harlem on Manhattan Island, certainly one of the early items in the literary history of that community. This was a forerunner of his great dendrological work six years later, wherein he systematically described American trees with all the vast paraphernalia of Latin terminology and with plates by his own hand. He became a forest-master under the King of Prussia, but never lost interest in his little Thuringian estate, which he called "America," where he could nurse the cuttings he had brought back in 1784.

Another man of science was the Reverend Frederick V. Melsheimer, a chaplain with the Brunswick dragoons. Wounded and taken prisoner at Bennington, he threw in his lot with the new country in 1779, and spent the remainder of his life as a Lutheran pastor in Pennsylvania. Of a scientific turn ever since his days at the University of Helmstedt, he devoted himself to the study of American insects. Indeed, his congregation sometimes had to wait when a handsome butterfly diverted him from the straight path to the morning service, and according to tradition he often preached with a beetle in his pocket. He published a *Coleoptera in Pennsylvania* (1806) in which he said, "To the best of my knowledge I have but few predecessors in the United States in this Understanding." This was certainly a modest statement; Thomas Say in his great descriptive work of 1824 recognized him as the father of American entomology. Whether or not the mercenaries brought in their fodder bags the Hessian fly which was to plague our farmers, they surely brought with them the science which alone could combat it.

In this long review of what the European armies carried out and back a hundred and fifty years ago, we have come upon some matters not commonly treated in the history textbooks. We look beneath gay military coats and brass and pipeclay and we see men, not mere fighting apparatus; even to soldiers war was not the sole concern. They like all the race were interested in the arts of getting along with other men, and of making life the richer and more lovely. The achievements of mankind in all these particulars are as significant to us as exploits upon the battle-field or compromises in the council chamber.

A SYNTHETIC PRINCIPLE IN
AMERICAN SOCIAL HISTORY

IT is interesting to look out upon a solemn congress
of historians; it seems distinguished by an eminent
dignity. The human mind learns by experience and
it may well regard with reverence those who know
the experience of the race, those who have learned
the lessons of history. These historians are society's
eyes of retrospection. The awestruck visitor mar-
vels at the wisdom that must have come from all
this searching. But if he listens long enough he will
be puzzled and disquieted by a question that, sooner
or later, is certain to be put. Someone will arise and
say with an air of immense profundity, "Ah, but
what is history?". There is soon discovered the
widest disagreement and, now disillusioned, the
visitor concludes that those who do not know what
history is can scarcely know its lessons. He may
think that a society which depends on organs of
retrospection that focus in so many different places
must be strabismic, or, in plain words, badly cross-
eyed.

"There stands Massachusetts," thundered Daniel
Webster in majestic phrase, "her past at least is

secure!" Had he been spared to read a shelf of histories by various authors by the name of Adams he would have realized that her past was not only insecure but quite defenseless. If history is constantly rearranging the past, it is now somewhat rearranging itself. Really, it is these uncertainties, these amiable disputes as to what history is, that make it at the moment a very live concern. Students flock to history classes because of rumors that adventures are there under way. Especially stirring is the new adventure of systematic social history, long contemplated and long preached, but tried as a subject of collegiate study chiefly in the past fifteen years. Classroom history, till lately, was supposed to deal with legal institutions and armed conflicts, and nowhere was this purview more generally accepted than in America, where the enormous task of building and maintaining forty-eight states in a federal union has attracted our historians especially into this political preoccupation.

Political historians have defended their monopoly by arguing that all the hopes and fears of man were ultimately registered in politics. Said one, thirty-seven years ago, "It is only through law and institutions that social forces become in a large sense operative." This exclusiveness was long since challenged by those who excavated the foundations of our economic life, and more recently have come others, brightly flaunting their modernity though really sprung from a forgotten ancestry in the eighteenth-century enlightenment, who claim an all-embracing breadth for history. Nothing that is human is alien to them, and some like J. H. Robinson are restive even under this implied restraint and discover fascinating interest in the social life of monkeys.

These social historians brand their elder brethren as mere specialists, crowding them into a corner. Outside the *leges,* civil and ecclesiastical, they contend are the *mores,* quasi-institutions like business corporations, colleges, trade unions and groupings quite unknown to law, societies to save humanity from one disaster or another, societies to cultivate a common taste. Guild socialists admonish us that these are what men live by and that politics, as generally understood, is obsolete. But beyond the sphere of organization are the folkways, unconscious but insistent social habits, currents of custom strong in the cumulative power of suggestion, against which only individuals with imagination and courage or, sometimes, sheer perversity, can make their way. In studying a people at a given time and place it is desirable to know the prevailing attitude of children toward their parents and vice versa. What was the public view of discipline, of pleasure, beauty, honesty, or thrift? A double standard in family relationships may deserve the historian's attention as much as a double standard in the currency. Mrs. Grundy may be more important than the President. There have been times when politics became a dominant concern, but most men in most times, and certainly most women, have paid it little personal attention. It has absorbed historians in part because it kept neat records. Always the man who leaves a diary or a treatise, or the group that leaves a minute book, figures disproportionately on the page of history.

Politics is interesting to most people as a game to watch, a conflict of wits, the stuff of drama. But its recreation in historical narrative, even when accomplished with due art, has seemed tedious to many because of its remoteness from the ordinary experience of life. Our leading manufacturer Mr. Ford believed that history as he had heard of it was not only unprofitable but vicious, tending as it did to exalt bloodshed and diplomatic cunning rather than the peaceful arts and the interests of the common life; he declared in his forceful way that it was not sound learning. Then with unflagging enterprise he gathered the physical remains of pre-machine days, with magic hand bodied forth long-vanished scenes in three-dimensional reality, revived old customs, and unwittingly proved himself one of the most enthusiastic and effective historians of our age. "If," wrote Emerson in his *Journal,* "we had a series of faithful portraits of private life in Egypt, Assyria, Greece and Rome, we might relinquish without a sigh their national annals." During the century since those words were penned, the historians of antiquity have more and more made such portraits their concern; this may be one reason for the increasing popularity of ancient history in recent years. History is a phase of life, the phase that is past but still operative in its influence. If one really ponders upon politics most of the time as he walks along the street, then he might well devote most of his historical study to politics. But if he thinks mostly of manners and morals, of arts and amusements, or of his own business, then is it not reasonable to study the history of these concerns?

By broadening its range, it seems, history will attract more readers. But the critic interrupts to say that anyone who did not wish to read of politics has long since had other histories to read, histories of medicine, of art, of science, of philosophy, to say nothing of the histories of religion and of economic effort. As time goes on successive groups of specialists achieve a high degree of self-consciousness and must have their histories; so there are under way histories of the public health movement, of paleontology, of organized sport. Strangely enough, all these have been acknowledged to be histories but not exactly history. To the orthodox a monograph on the development of medicine in Michigan would not have been regarded as eligible material, a monograph on Indian warfare would. To say that all this is changing suggests that general history seems to some, now rather more than formerly, a practicable human achievement.

General history implies that we can generalize. It is not the history of little groups but of great masses, and supposes, therefore, that the mass can feel a common impulse, think a common thought, perform a common act. It suggests, at least ideally, that there is some relation between medical history and art history and economic history and the rest, that in each may be exhibited common human traits and common human progress or at any rate common human change. It resembles natural science in counting on a certain degree of regularity. What was typical and what was singular? asks the scholar as he reads biography and local history; the typical is interesting as the very staple of general history, the singular as illustrating the fact of aberration in the human race. As with the scientist the data are widely various and infinitely numerous and the judgment must be keen as to what constitutes a proper sample. Like science general history examines all the data it can find, with Baconian faith that out of subconsciousness some sort of explanation will suggest itself. If the faith is justified, with this second stage mere industry gives way to scholarship; the historian sets out to check his guess, and laboriously month after month, perhaps year after year, tries to fit great quantities of new facts into his suggested pattern. If perchance they seem to fit, lifted by a dizzy and a dangerous elation, he announces a principle of synthesis, an interpretation. Then, tragically, ninety-nine times out of a hundred, nothing happens. His evidence turns out to be so meager he can not get even a passing attention for his brave conclusions, unless they be so wondrously bizarre that for a moment he must endure a prominence in public ridicule. Fortunately there is a hundredth chance that he may have hit on something that others can take seriously, or at least find useful as suggesting an approach in historical investigation.

The fact is that the reading public would rather have the writer take the risk. It wants, as it might say, to make some head and tail out of this so-called social history. Every undergraduate has read a certain history of the people of the United States properly considered in a large sense the pioneer work in this enormous field. It showed how many, many things outside the scope of politics were affected with a human and therefore an historical interest, presented them oftentimes with vivid picturesqueness, and spaded into light many kinds of forgotten source material, notably long-buried files of newspapers. It will, therefore, permanently stand as one of the significant works in our historiography. But to the modern reader it seems more like a giant notebook than a history; if there is design he does not easily discover it. One topic after another is interestingly illustrated, not discussed; it seems as if the author published whatever he had chanced to find on one topic after another, never rejecting a bright fact even though it had but little value in any conceivable mosaic, never waiting to find the little necessary bits of evidence to make a picture that told something definite; the sketches were stuck one to another in the row by transition sentences oftentimes so strangely adventitious as to bring a smile even to the most appreciative.

The reader wants philosophy if he can get it, which is another way of saying that he wants arrangement that leaves him with an idea. It scarcely needs be said that he is making an exorbitant demand. H. T. Buckle thought it could be met, though with difficulty, and roundly scolded historians in general because they had not tried to meet it. Recalling that the expectation of regularity in nature had long since become an article of faith with men of science he said, "If the same expectation is not generally found among historians, it must be ascribed partly to their being of inferior ability to the investigators of nature, and partly to the greater complexity of those social phenomena with which their studies are concerned." He found the key in the influence of environment upon society, not only upon economic but upon æsthetic, religious, political, and other human interests. The anthropogeographers have followed in his train—we in America are recently familiar with the climate thesis of Professor Huntington—but they have usually known the geographical stage rather better than the historical drama which they allege it has so drastically conditioned. Hegel, at the other extreme, found the determinant in a world spirit working for the despot in the ancient Orient, for the "dominant order" in the classical age, and for man as a free being in modern times. Not greatly different in its processional quality was the culture-epoch theory that all societies must rise through stages like an individual. Spengler carries it a little farther; what true history should show is the growth of a society into civilization and then a hardening and decay. Not greatly different in the sense of destiny was the Christian theory first summed up by Augustine that God had willed the rise and fall of successive empires as a preliminary exercise to establishing the city of perfection. Much modern history, formerly political but lately upon many themes, arranges itself to exhibit the overpowering growth of nationalism. Then, too, since Heeren's time a popular theory of history has been that most things, at least within historic time, got done by reason of the economic motive functioning in the struggle between self-conscious groups. That this scheme, dangerous in ordinary hands, can be used with sanity and restraint, is illustrated in the Beards' *Rise of American Civilization;* it is that conception which gives unity and organization to the book. Others can tell us the really significant history of the world in terms of education, of agriculture, of architecture, or of literature.

Any general history that is more than a heap of data or a collection of little monographic pamphlets haply bound within a single pair of covers must adopt some principle or principles of synthesis. "Truth," wrote St. Thomas Aquinas, "is the adequation of the thing and the understanding." Facts are useful only if they tell us something. In writing general history it may be better to build on a wrong thesis than on none at all. "Truth," observes another philosopher, Lord Bacon, "emerges more readily from error than from confusion."

We have been speaking of the general historians as if they constituted a considerable class. Really there are very few with such Gargantuan appetite that they claim all creation for their feast. Most of

[86]

those who seek to set in order the multiplied complexities of modern times are content with one form of civilization, indeed more often with the experience of a single people or section or county. Others even within this narrower field confine intensive study to one period, one phase, one human interest or one occupation, but with new purpose and new spirit. Histories of medicine by doctors, of law by lawyers, of art by critics, are from our point of view written by untrained amateurs. The qualified historian knows less of the technique and problems of the specialty he writes upon, but from much previous study he knows more of human relations in times past. He writes of medicine not as an art but as a group function, how and why communities supported their physicians, what they had in common with lawyers, clergymen and other people and how their influence was different, their methods of recruitment, their professional discipline, the degree of their authority and control, in short the interplay of physicians and society.

In these remarks much has been said of general history, though in the sodality of those pledged to its service the term is seldom used. Rather, one hears of social history, which may or may not mean the same. The fact is that the social historian, though this may not be believed, is oftentimes a practically minded person. Realizing how much has been done in political and military history he tends, for the present, without resigning theoretical claims, to neglect them. Those parts of ecclesiastical, economic, or literary history which have been well done likewise call him less insistently; though, as has been suggested, he is constantly concerned with their interrelations. In the actual gathering of original materials he is more likely to be found reaping fields not much invaded before by competent historical scholarship. Due to this fact, one comes on classifications of historical interests as political, military, ecclesiastical, and what not, winding up with social history as a synonym for miscellaneous or nondescript. In this mistaken view the social historian seems permanently a specialist in curiosities rather than a man of science seeking by the study of the past to discover and then to present in systematic form how societies have behaved. Actually, into whatever strange bypaths he wanders, he carries in his pocket a rough tentative sketch-map of the entire country to which as he is able he adds his emendations.

As you have long since suspected, the social historian is often the victim of a secret bias toward simplicity. He is apt to think that he can find one principle of synthesis into which everything can be jammed. A sociologist, long nourished on principles, who borrows history, is likely thus to rummage the past for illustrations, rather more than the historian, trained to respect facts in themselves, who borrows the point of view of sociology. The sane historian soon finds that he can not explain all that a society has done by what it has had to eat or by its tools or by rainfall or soil exhaustion or topography. As any child would say, a number of things have to be taken into account. Nevertheless in this pluralistic interpretation he wants to take as few of them as possible. Among the few principles he takes, that which enables him to give meaning to the greatest number of facts is the best. The Beards, to return to one enterprise, have thought that the conflict of groups, especially groups in economic competition, afforded a good principle of design for the exposition of American social history, but actually and properly they have decorated the borders of this picture with much matter quite as interesting as the elements within. Judged by the canon of inclusiveness it is a principle which would not satisfy all historians even as the most available. But it is certainly more satisfying than the Marxist principle, which assumes that most men most of the time are trying to do somebody else out of property; it further assumes that those who contemplate the same victim tend to work together, that more historic facts can be explained or related on this principle than on any other, and that there-

[89]

fore as a touchstone of significance it suggests the best scheme for the presentation of history. If with all this many will disagree, upon them rests the burden of finding another or a few other principles.

In dealing with American history one notices that different times have different dominant ideas; now it is the growing national consciousness, now the desire for cultural independence, now democracy, now submission to urban standards, now the insistence upon social control in place of *laissez faire*. Yielding no worship to an Hegelian *Zeitgeist,* we may roughly periodize American history according to these dominants, well realizing, however, that each must share its power with other contemporary ideas only less imposing. Yet there is a general sense of growth in culture, or at least in civilization. How can the growth of any given time be measured? The physical community grows simply larger and can be gauged as by successive rings; but civilization itself grows in the mode of evolution, constantly dividing and subdividing functions toward greater and greater complexity.

Suppose a community of men and women, who unlike primitive folk are tolerant of social change, isolated on a distant but opulent island and growing only by natural increase. In this case civilization would soon bear a rough ratio to numbers. Most men, themselves concerned with the fundamental problem of staying alive, might be willing to support a specialist who could relieve them of supplementary worries, a single specialist who would counsel them on their relations to the spirit world, on their relations with each other, on their health, on the perception and expression of beauty, and on many other things. Someone would try it, and if he found social support, the variety would become permanent through the intellectual propagation of successors. As the community grew, one such specialist would not be enough and support would be furnished others up to a certain number. If more tried it than the community needed, the marginal professionals, of course, would have to perish.

Some learned man, we may imagine, feels more interest and competence in the health province of his domain; he abandons his other responsibilities and, if conditions are friendly, survives as a specialist in that field alone. That is to say, he has discovered that the community has here and there, with the growth of numbers, such a fair continuity of problems of this sort as to pay for his living by their solution. Ultimately he creates successors by example or by casual training. Another experimental variation has become a permanent variety. The doctor has branched off the professional stem, as the clergyman, the teacher, the artist and the lawyer may soon do as well. The full recognition of

[91]

the permanent profession comes with the establishment of an institution for formal training. Up to
the last stage all that we have said applies as well
to crafts or skills.

But the evolution of professional species has only
now begun. In the Boston *Gazette,* February 6,
1738, Peter Pelham advertised that he taught
"Dancing, Writing, Reading, painting upon Glass,
and all kinds of needle work"; he was a painter, an
engraver and also gave instruction on the harpsi-
chord and in the elements of psalmody. It will be
noticed that he was a functionary but partly differentiated; he was not a farmer, a seafaring man,
a clergyman, a doctor, or a lawyer, it is true, but he
contained within himself the rudimentary beginnings of half a dozen specialists. Really, that society of 1738 did not have sufficient occasion for
him in all these varied forms of competence to keep
him alive and he had to piece out as a merchant
of tobacco. Eventually there would be engravers,
dancing masters, painters, musicians, various teachers of elementary subjects including manual training, who could trace back the converging lines of
their respective developments to such an unforked
stem of their general branch.

So, too, one sees the printer in the course of time
throw off the editor, the publisher, the advertising
man; the clergyman develop special functionaries

like the college professor, the missionary, the religious teacher, the social worker and the like; the doctor, indulging one of his interests, produce the naturalist; and the naturalist break up into the geologist, the botanist, the chemist, to say nothing of the later petrologist, histologist and the rest. Institutions parallel all this differentiation. In 1800 one theatre program might offer Hamlet, a farce and a hornpipe; while in 1900 these three forms of entertainment are found in three different theatres, just as the old general store has become a half a dozen different kinds of stores. As in biological evolution the mother type may itself persist—the printer, the clergyman, and the doctor we have noticed are examples—or contrasting with the biological process the undifferentiated type, as in the case of the general naturalist, may almost vanish.

Sometimes, if the botanists will allow the figure, a twig from a humbler bush works its way up to join some shoot from the professional tree to form a new branch. When Asher Benjamin published *The Country Builder's Assistant* at Greenfield, Massachusetts, in 1797, he described himself as a "housewright." Then he mixed with artists for a season. On the title page of his *American Builder's Companion* (Boston, 1805) he appears as "architect and carpenter," in his work of 1830 he presents himself as "architect," one of the first men of

American training thus to make such a professional claim. By the same anastomosis from the farrier and the doctor, as we might illustrate, came the veterinary surgeon; from another kind of doctor's interest joining with one of the barber's actually came the dentist. We can see the undertaker breaking upward from the joiner who specialized in building coffins, sometimes with precise date as the traveler John Lambert records at Charleston in 1807, but no really scientific interest bent down to join him and he remains and flourishes in the space between the trades and the professions. All this is not mere speculation but the common facts of record. It does not offer a theory of social history, if such a thing were conceivable, but a scheme of organizing social history.

In the history of civilization, if not the history of culture, the degree of differentiation is one measure of maturity. The community's knowledge and competence is advanced in particulars by specialization. The community that insists on each individual acquiring all he needs by personal experience must be satisfied with less than one which trusts the expert. The Old South had among its planters an attractive culture, but in so far as it failed to develop various professionals and imported its art, its science, its literature, its collegiate education, it was a dependent province in a larger civilization, though it made its characteristic contribution of certain experts, such as planters, statesmen, and military men.

A certain complicated civilization may be less distinguished in some forms of culture than a certain simpler one. It may be that the present-day Americans, highly differentiated, can not rival the Greeks in sculpture. If so, one asks the reason for this fact as he traces out the evolution of the species in this climate, as he watches John Frazee, a Jerseyman who lettered gravestones, and Hezekiah Augur, a clever carver of ships' figure-heads in New Haven, a little more than a century ago, slowly turning into pioneer sculptors of portrait busts. What delayed that branching? On the other hand what hurried the differentiation of characteristic American types, the lawyer-politician, the college administrator, the dentist, the planter and the rest? How far was the disparity in social evolution between North and South responsible for the Civil War? It is surprising how much that we recognize as the stuff of social history can be related to this theme-plot of social evolution, using the word as the biologists use it to describe the process of differentiation.

Actually, the isolated people we imagined, where social evolution proceeds so neatly of itself, does not exist and has not for many centuries. In the

[95]

contacts of the world there has operated the multiform example of other communities; carriers, conscious or unconscious, have brought suggestion toward new interests, new needs, new specialties. A colonial society has memories that quicken differentiation along the lines well known at home. A young community easily reached from one older and more mature receives adventurous specialists so fast that it has little need to invent them if it could. Indeed, they are likely to come too fast and many die of inanition. Civilization in transit in such a case is more active than civilization in natural evolution. If we return to our figure of the tree, these chance influences from outside, these winds from the east, have been constantly tending to graft on new branchlets, many times successfully, where they might or might not have grown in time themselves. Conditions of environment or new apparatus as well as such chance importations may encourage the growth and differentiation of some branches much faster than others.

It is the claim of this paper that the concept of social evolution, with due attention to such modifications, offers an available scheme on which to bring an immense number of seemingly discrete facts into an understandable relation. How far and in what way did any influence check or accelerate social evolution? How did social evolution produce the dominant ideas we talked of as marking certain times and, more important, how far was it modified by them in turn? This scheme does not explain facts, but brings many of them into relation, which is what the social historian really wants. It does not integrate everything; much has to be hung on other racks. For instance, some of the folkways we mentioned some time since are but distantly related to it. But it can be of greater aid than most writers of social history have noticed. It brings together the history of Connecticut and the history of Colorado. A kinetic principle, it helps make social history more than a series of panoramic culture pictures; it helps make of it a living whole.

REFUSE IDEAS AND THEIR DISPOSAL

THE professor whose daily morning walk is through the central thoroughfare of Harlem passes the studies and consulting rooms of certain other scholars—Zangar the Mysterious, Mme. Futura and their colleagues who, for an appropriate fee, will read your fate in the position of the stars. The professor, pondering as he walks, recalls that it was an income as a practical astrologer which enabled Johann Kepler to exist while he worked out the elliptic pathway of the planets; that his great master, Tycho Brahe, had concerned himself with horoscopes and prophecy; that Huygens, the improver of the telescope, and a host of other scientists of early modern times, had been serious students of this planetary influence on the destinies of individual men. On arriving at the university, he finds there no teacher of judicial astrology. Kepler and the others are nowhere more revered, but it is in spite of these concerns. The learning of the university has long since cast out this astrologic lore; it still exists, but it now lurks ignominiously in the shadowy hallways of One Hundred and Twenty Fifth Street.

[99]

At the beginning of the nineteenth century the physicians of America, from the great Benjamin Rush, of Philadelphia, to the fledgling doctor newly certified to practise in the smallest village, used the lancet and the leech freely and with confidence. The letting off of blood would relieve the plethoric, upon the one hand, or restore swifter action to the anæmic, upon the other. It was realized that the remedy might be overdone—perhaps too much vital fluid had been taken from the dying Washington—but it was a very general resort in almost every kind of malady, a proceeding, as a writer in the *Medical Repository* for 1806 (X, 13) remarked, "the most eligible in point of ease, safety, decency and agreeableness." To-day it may be found, but, with a few exceptions such as certain operations on the eye, it flourishes only with old wives slyly practicing among the ignorant. As the *British Medical Journal* (May 27, 1911) solemnly observes, "what is called quackery at the present day often represents what was orthodox medicine two or three centuries ago."

Young Americans, in the early days of the republic, got their knowledge of the world from new-fangled textbooks called geographies, notably those produced by Dr. Jedidiah Morse, a leading scholar of Massachusetts. More than a score of his editions had spread through the country by 1820. In his

Geography Made Easy (ed. 1800) he presents some
fascinating natural history:

> Grey Squirrels sometimes migrate in considerable
> numbers. If in their course they meet with a river, each
> of them takes a shingle, piece of bark, or the like, and
> carries it to the water; thus equipped they embark, and
> erect their tails to the gentle breeze, which soon wafts
> them over in safety; but a sudden flaw of wind some-
> times produces a disastrous shipwreck.

This dramatic picture, it is pleasant to remark, has
not wholly passed out of literature, but one finds it
now not in accepted texts by scholars correspond-
ing in prestige to Dr. Morse, but in illustrated
nursery books like *The Tale of Squirrel Nutkin,* so
cherished along with Peter Rabbit by tiny listeners
four years of age. With the growth of knowledge
and the critical spirit, what once was science has
now sunk into the lore of bedtime stories.

Not so long ago, as historic time is reckoned,
writers on the almost universal art of agriculture
credited the moon with a determining influence on
the fields, from seeding-time to harvest; Sir William Herschel, about a century since, gave the force
of his mighty name to support the doctrine. In re-
tentive rustic minds remote from academic contacts, it still persists sufficiently to warrant a careful
confutation by the meteorological physicist of our

federal government but a few years ago, but he finds no contemporary Herschels to oppose him. Robert Boyle, the pioneer of modern chemistry, believed in the efficacy of certain amulets; they still are worn, but not by scientists. The most conspicuous figure before him, Paracelsus, found an intellectual interest and considerable profit in the manufacture of love philtres, one of the earliest applications of chemical engineering. If the daily papers are to be believed, they are yet purchased by the ill-informed and self-distrustful, but the principles of their construction are not taught in colleges.

It would be wearisome to recount such illustrations further. Across the memory of the historian float hundreds like them which, in their total, richly authorize a generalization. It may be stated in a metaphor: The cast-off garments of the intellectuals of one age are found, albeit soiled and ragged, on the backs of the ignorant many in the next.

In time the new light from above, slowly sifting through the strata of society, reveals their poverty and tawdriness and they are finally thrown away by everybody. Take, as a single instance, the old analysis of matter as a composition of earth, air, fire and water. This simple formula which had satisfied Aristotle and the other scholars of antiquity, survived into what we call the modern era, survived the period of discovery and first settling of America. Our early colonial writers of a scientific turn accepted it without a question. But retorts and test tubes, ceaseless in their revelations across the sea, slowly broke up matter into many parts, and by the beginning of the nineteenth century some forty elements were known. It is interesting, then, to find Samuel Thomson, of Maine, in his *Narrative,* which after its original publication in 1819 ran through many editions, founding a system of medicine upon the old conception; somewhat earlier had appeared in New York an anonymous treatise entitled *A Physical Enquiry into the Origin and Causes of the Pestilential Fever* (1798) that accepted the old four elements, adding two, "electron" and "mother," for good measure. But such expositions were heartily derided by the medical profession; they were branded as anachronistic. We witness here a proceeding familiar in the history of knowledge; an old, worn-out idea was being kicked down for good through the trap-door into the void below, to be remembered only by the antiquarians. Sometimes such notions, as they are discarded, leave traces in the language. "Temperament," "humor," and many of the adjectives that go with them, are examples. The name of Antiphlogistine, a patent medicine, bears the print of the old doctrine of phlogiston as the principle of fire. Sometimes one leaves a graphic fossil, as it were,

like the common astrological picture on the alma-
nacs of the zodiacal signs pointing to the gentleman
so courteously exposing his viscera in the interest
of public instruction.

Since the later Middle Ages, Christendom has
been accustomed to seek light in colleges and universities. Americans so far as they have paid respect to learning at all have honored it in this as-
sociation; among the first transactions on this soil
was the establishment of such a seminary as might
school their leaders. Few enterprises in the natural
history of ideas will more attract the modern
scholar than the enquiry as to the tone and type of
academic thinking in this country from the beginning to the present. What has happened to the
certitudes of college classrooms—not merely to
"facts" which have been definitely superseded by
more information, but to the basic conceptions of
the academic mind? Let us take our point of observation in those years that closed the eighteenth
century and began the century that followed.

The atmosphere in those American academic
halls must first be sensed. It was religious: largely,
indeed, ecclesiastical, almost as much so as in the
seminary on the heights of Quebec or in the royal
and pontifical university of the city of Mexico.
Throughout the score of colleges that then existed
there was an air of piety, from the general prayers

at six in the morning to the general prayers at night.
In such an environment, it will readily be realized,
the things of this world were not allowed to en-
croach too far upon those of the spirit. Sacred
history was immeasurably more important than
profane; in the Yale College library the student
who succeeded in getting in could find ten separate
works upon the fall of man, but no copy of the
great book on the *Decline and Fall of the Roman
Empire.* "My book was on every table," wrote Edward Gibbon in his *Autobiography;* "the historian
was crowned by the taste and fashion of the day."
He probably did not know it, but he was not
crowned by the taste and fashion of New Haven.
The teachers in that institution were churchmen
first and scholars afterward. It is interesting to note
the formal reception of Benjamin Silliman in
1799, as remembered by Noah Porter: "After
prayers, the call from the President—*sedete omnes*
—brought us all upon our seats, when Mr. Silliman, at a signal from the President, rose and read
a written formula declaring his assent to the West-
minster Catechism and the Saybrook Platform. So
he was inducted into the Tutorship." Under such
auspices came into academic life one who was to be
the greatest American scientist of his day. The college might at that time have been somewhat less a
training school for ministers than formerly—only

one-fourth of the graduates of Yale now went into the clergy as compared with one-half two generations before—but the interest of the faculty had not greatly changed.

The American college president was, in the language of biology, a throw-off from the clergyman, and at the end of the eighteenth century he was very imperfectly detached. More than nine-tenths, by actual count, of the college presidents in office during the forty years after 1790 were ordained ministers, and they saw life from the sacred desk quite as steadily after their induction as before. The professors, a scant half-hundred at the turning of the century, who in the evolution of American professional species were throw-offs from the president, like him, preponderantly, were clerical in caste and training. The faculty of the Western University of Pennsylvania (1822), where the local clergy of the town of Pittsburgh were the staff complete, presented an extreme example. Of the twenty officers appointed to give instruction in Columbia College during the first three decades after the Revolution, twelve were clergymen and all but three of these so distinguished themselves in that calling as to earn doctorates in theology. This becomes more striking when we reflect that of the five hundred and fifty, or so, who now hold professorial appointments under that corporation scarcely one has such a doctorate.

To understand the mental attitude of academic men of that day, however, one must remember not only that they cherished a religious system but that they knew that their system was being challenged. It was a time—and the present-day professor feels a twinge of sympathy for his bewildered predecessors—it was a time of youth in revolt. At the beginning of the period the shadow of the Revolutionary War was not yet dispelled, the after-shadow of ethical confusion which all wars leave behind them. It was observed that drunkenness increased among the young, and vice was thought to stalk more brazenly. The Reverend William Bentley, the charming diarist of Salem, decided to remain a bachelor when he learned by chance that the lady of his choice, like her friends, could use a kind of language that he had overheard before only among sailors. Soon girls began to bob their hair (an indiscretion they were wont to hide by wigs and turbans after they had changed their minds) and to wear dresses which they called sensible but clergymen called scandalous and doctors said gave no protection and were dangerous to health. It was a time of trouble for official guardians of youth, neither the first nor the last.

The winds of revolutionary doctrine blowing from the Paris faubourgs brought infection to increase the malady. The ancient decencies were rudely questioned. What the fathers said was order, the sons declared was tyranny; what the sons extolled as liberty, the fathers branded anarchy pure and simple. France was calling "her daughter America," rapturously wrote Citizen Brackenridge of Pennsylvania in 1793. But there were others who heard the cry with terror. "Your Sans Culottes are few and contemptible," wrote the President of Dickinson College to a Scottish friend in disgust, "ours are almost the Majority of the People." French manners, French songs, French amusements came with French politics and, worst of all, French infidelity, which enforced a trend toward deism already well begun. Many students at the staid old colleges of Yale and Princeton took the names of favorite European rationalists and used them in preference to their own. It was thought, though probably in error, that students and others were widely copying that aggressive anti-clerical organization, the Bavarian Illuminati. The old historians of Harvard, Bowdoin, Williams and other institutions record with shame the decline of pious faith in the generation which flourished in the last years of the eighteenth century. The number of professing Christians in the colleges dropped to

[108]

almost nothing. It was a time to call forth the greatest intellectual effort that the academic minds could make. They put their best thought on the record; we can watch their mental processes as if under a microscope. We can mark some of their ideas, as a laboratory scientist would color certain tissues for close observation, and then watch how they have fared under the wear and tear of time.

One quality of thought immediately arrests attention: their complete dependence on the Holy Scripture as a book of history and science and an infallible index of what the future had in store. They reasoned that they lived in an extraordinary time, a time of great significance in the Christian epic and hence undoubtedly noticed in the Bible, the Work which had the unique property of being a true narrative of the future as well as the past. "Prophecy," explained Dr. John H. Livingston, the most famous president of Rutgers College, in a sermon seventy-two pages long, "Prophecy is furnished like history with a chronological calendar, and the predictions with respect to the time of their accomplishment, may be referred to three distinct classes," those definitely dated, either in literal or symbolic numbers, those related to other events in an indicated order, and those in which no time relation is mentioned.

The Old Testament, they declared, was a veritable almanac of prophecy. Scholars had sought in the first part of the Bible premonition of the great events recorded in the last, but now they searched the Scripture to learn the sequel of the ominous transactions of their own day, especially in Europe, though the defeat of the Federalists in 1800 was numbered too with the catastrophes. As remarked in 1810 by Dr. Morse, sometime tutor in Yale and then the most influential minister of Massachusetts, the events of the last twenty years constrained men to believe that God was "preparing the world for some grand revolution, some wonderful display of his sovereign and almighty power." Perhaps if they could not stay the raging fire about them they might discover that it soon would cease. They knew they were destined to conquer the world some time; perhaps the victory was imminent. They were not disappointed in their search. "My brethren," said President Griffin of Williams College, "it is too near the dawn of those happier times for your pious enterprise to fail." What was the dawn so eagerly anticipated? Nothing less than the beginning of the millennium.

Disturbed by the "jacobinical phrensy" all around them, the devout were gathered in the meetinghouses for social prayer and to listen to long exegeses on the prophets by such authorities as Timothy Dwight, the President of Yale. Let us glance at this extraordinary figure. He was the most conspicuous man in New England; he was the leading academic man in the United States. We see him mount the pulpit to deliver an address on the Fourth of July, 1798. He is six feet tall, portly, dignified and personable. He is playfully referred to as "The Pope of New England," and he jokes familiarly with friends about the triple crown he is supposed to wear. He is a celebrated controversialist, a man of varied learning, the ideal scholar of his time. As he speaks his rich and solemn voice penetrates the heart of every hearer. He expounds the sixteenth chapter of Revelation, where the seven angels take the vials the beast has given them and each in turn pours out the wrath of God upon the unrepentant world, and noisome, grievous sores, fountains of blood, scorching fire and divers uncleannesses plague the soul of man. The real pouring of the seven vials, President Dwight explains, began about 800 A. D., when the Pontiff of the Romish Church essayed to crown a civil ruler. Four had been emptied when Martin Luther nailed his theses to the chapel door. This gives the time consumed by each as one hundred and eighty years, and by this reckoning mankind in 1798 stands more than half way through the pouring of the sixth. Premonitory agitations are about them— the castigation of the Romish Church upon the one hand, the temporary rise of infidelity upon the other. It is not long until the Antichristian Kingdom will finally fall. Let us do what we can to mitigate the horrors about us—shall our daughters become the concubines of the Illuminati? Shall our sons become the dragoons of the followers of Marat? Let us hasten to prepare the world for the divine event. "Almost all judicious commentators," he says later, "have agreed that the Millennium, in the full and perfect sense, will begin at a period not far from the year 2000 A. D."

Why the year 2000? Dr. William Linn, for three years Acting President of Rutgers, makes this clear by an exposition of Daniel. The drama of terrestrial existence, like the prologue of creation, lasts for seven days, but a day is as a thousand years; hence the final scene will begin six thousand years after God said, Let there be Light. Dr. Eliphalet Nott, the President of Union, speaking in 1806, explains it further: "In the economy of redemption four thousand years are spent in preparing the way for the introduction of Messiah, the birth of Christ. Two thousand more in vanquishing his enemies, and fixing the boundaries of his empire." Then the millennium; "Christians are now, perhaps generally, united in the opinion that the Messiah is yet to reign a thousand years on the earth."

But these scholars turned also to Revelation, that

book replete with mystic wisdom. Daniel had spoken of the prevailing of the terrible fourth beast for a time and times and a dividing of time (Dan. vii, 25) ; this was echoed in the Apocalypse where the woman was secluded in the wilderness for a time, times and half a time (Rev. xii, 14). But this, wrote Dr. Linn, was symbolically the same period as that indicated in the three and a half days during which the bodies of the two puissant witnesses lay outside the great city where the beast had slain them (Rev. xi, 9). Now a day *may* be a lunar day— that is, a space of thirty years—which would make their sojourn outside the walls one hundred and five years in length; but more probably it is as a year of years, by which reckoning three and a half times three hundred and sixty totals twelve hundred and sixty years, the period whose end must mark the dawn of the millennium.

In this case much depended on when those years began. "It is now generally admitted," wrote President Griffin of Williams, "that the grand period of 1260 'times' or years, assigned by Daniel and John for the continuance of the papal church, and papal kingdoms, and the Mahometan delusion, commenced in 606 (the year that the pastor of Rome was declared universal bishop and the Arabian impostor retired to the cave of Hera to construct his koran) and that it will terminate in 1866, or, if you reckon in Chaldaic years, in 1847 or 8." A Chaldaic year was three hundred and sixty days (or, in prophetic concept, years) ; since Daniel lived among the Chaldeans and must have used their system, that without doubt was the reckoning to take. After 1848 there still would be two short periods before the full millennium, which would come in the twentieth century. Seventy weeks—that is, seventy prophetic weeks of seven years each—was a period of symbolic significance, recalled President Livingston, as he instanced the four hundred and ninety years between the decree of Artaxerxes, legally establishing the Jewish religion, and the death of Christ. Now the angel must begin his flight after the Reformation and before the fall of Antichrist, therefore between 1500 and 2000. The signs of the times, he said, show that he has begun it now, probably starting seventy prophetic weeks after 1500, i. e. 1790, when the most virulent of the current disorders had had their rise.

The year 2000, though supported by a large number of college teachers, was not universally accepted. President Griffin was willing to consider 1921; President Linn declared his choice for 1916; Professor McKnight, who filled the spacious chair of Moral Philosophy, Logic, Rhetoric and Belles Lettres at Columbia, found evidence for 1900; Dr. John B. Romeyn, an alumnus and a trustee of that institution and a man whom two colleges vainly sought as president, expected the beginning about 1860; other writers, too, felt that by 1813, when Napoleon, who probably was Antichrist, was ravishing Europe, the present era had entered on its last half-century. One clergyman, forgetting prudence, wrote in 1795 predicting the grand event for the following spring. This David Austin had a penchant for applying prophecy too nearly; he found in the Scriptures a promise that Thomas Jefferson would not be elected President, but there was an error in his exegesis. Whatever may have been his personal outlook, he had the happy fortune, apparently, of having a shrewd wife. Here is a passage in his work on *The Voice of God to the People of the United States:* "Of these things I spake to Mrs. Austin. She said an ingenious mind might spiritualize anything."

The public statements of the academic leaders were crowded with the awful imagery of Revelation, the woman with the eagle's wings, the seven-headed dragon, the strange composite beasts—a fauna all unknown to nature—the man of sin, "the old serpent called the Devil," and the shining Bride of the Lamb. The Roman Church, as has been intimated, was revealed to them as a central element of error and disaster. Was it not of great significance, asked President Linn, that the beast's

[115]

number and that of this Church were the same if worked out in the proper numerals of the Greek alphabet? Was it not a striking coincidence that *Vicarius Filii Dei,* a title which the Pope had assumed, could be developed to the same result? Supernatural agents were working all about the Christian:

> Angels and ministers of grace defending him
> And imps in eager caucus raffling for his soul.

These were not mere figures of speech. "Yesterday," writes Charles Brockden Brown in 1801, "in the morning we went to church, and heard Dr. Dwight preach an ingenious sermon to prove the reality of good and bad angels, or genii." Nothing was portrayed in sacred writing but had positive existence exactly as described. The New England of Timothy Dwight was not entirely unlike the New England of Cotton Mather, a hundred years before.

The new enterprises of orthodox Christianity— the Bible societies, foreign missionary societies, abolition societies, and the like, factors in the counter-reformation against Unitarianism—were hailed as harbingers of the millennium. At the same time the impending dawn made necessary a redoubled effort if the preparations were to be completed. It all seemed fated, and yet requiring the coöperation of the human will. When one reflected that there were eight hundred million souls on earth and only sixty million Protestants, it was obvious that fifty years or a hundred or even two hundred was a short time. Missions must be prosecuted with great vigor to effect their object. Timothy Dwight did not state precisely what the earth would look like during the millennium, "when the Romish cathedral, the mosque, and the pagoda, shall not have one stone left upon another," but it is fairly clear from his context that he would be satisfied if the traveler around the world would find one great continuous New England. In 1823, Dr. Francis Wayland, soon to be President of Brown, preaching on the missionary enterprises, was willing to admit Scotland as a model as well: "In a word, point to the loveliest village that smiles upon a Scottish or New-England landscape and compare it with the filthiness and brutality of a Cafferian kraal, and we tell you that our object is to render the Cafferian kraal as happy and gladsome as that Scottish or New-England village."

The millennium itself, "in the economy of redemption," was to be a thousand years, the reign of Christ on earth. After this there was to be a short period of distress, a woeful time when Satan should be loosed a little season, and then the last judgment (Rev. xx). But what were a thousand years? They might be prophetic years of years, thought Professor McKnight, making 365,000 (or 360,000) in all, so long a period as to seem virtually eternity. In this case the judgment would probably precede, and the wicked be cast down with Satan at the beginning. Dr. Eliphalet Nott and others showed their belief in this and feared that the verse about the Devil's inning had been misinterpreted. At any rate the world would not wait long to learn the truth.

Where did these leading American academic men get all these ideas? They were not new; they were not American in origin. Great respect was paid in sermons to the treatises of Joseph Mede, a scholar at the University of Cambridge in early Stuart times, especially his great work on the Apocalypse. There was frequent reference, too, to Thomas Newton (1704–1782), Bishop of Bristol, whose three-volume *Dissertations on the Prophecies* had reached their eleventh edition in 1794. Alexander Fraser's *Key to the Prophecies,* originally published in Edinburgh in 1795 and soon reprinted in Philadelphia, made an impression on Dr. Livingston and others. But the greatest influence was wielded by George Stanley Faber (1777–1854), who had made his reputation at Oxford in 1799 by two sermons on the seven vials. His first extensive works, issued in 1807 and 1808, were promptly republished in Boston and gained wide distribution. He continued to expound the same great themes for nearly half a century, but his audience dwindled.

If the study of prophecy showed scripturalism in its extreme form, there were other manifestations almost as striking. The habit of industry might be recommended to the young on many grounds, but the modern counsellor would not rate his reasons as did Dr. Samuel Stanhope Smith, the President of Princeton; in his commencement address of 1797 on this theme he put foremost that it was enjoined upon us by the Bible. A college president to-day might work out a conclusive argument as to the imprudence of gambling, but his reasoning would not take the same course as did that of Provost John M. Mason, charged with the conduct of Columbia. He explained that the Scriptures sanctioned the use of the lot for only two occasions, the choice of a civil ruler and the disposition of property. Games of chance, then, were not specified; to refer such unauthorized matters to lot was impious, because it implied a planless universe, an insult to an omniscient God. If the player's finances were disturbed by his devotion to cards, that was not in itself a reason for giving up the practice; it was merely the way God took to evidence his displeasure at such a conception of cosmology as the player obviously entertained, a conception contrary to the Scripture.

Professor Moses Stuart, of Andover Seminary, preached before the Female Charitable Society of Salem in 1815, taking as his text Deuteronomy xv, 11: "I command thee saying, thou shalt open thy hand wide unto thy brother, to the poor, and to the needy of the land." He began the sermon, "The duty of giving alms is plainly and positively enjoined, both in the Old Testament and the New." Christians should be charitable because they are told to be. But already, even in Massachusetts, men were making a different approach to ethical problems. A few years before, Dr. John Prince had preached before the same society from Proverbs xxii, 2: "The rich and the poor meet together; the Lord is the maker of them all." His first sentence is no less significant in its contrast to Professor Stuart's: "The system of nature presented to the mind of man, affords a wonderful field for contemplation."—the system of nature, not the literal command of God.

So much for certain ideas prevalent in academic circles at the beginning of the nineteenth century. It will be noted that the American writers we have quoted were no obscure eccentrics, no ignorant itinerants haranguing rude frontiersmen, but the scholarly leaders of their generation, the official predecessors of such men as President Angell, President Butler and President Dodds. Calling to mind our general thesis, let us turn to see what happened to these ideas. When Napoleon was safely taken off to St. Helena and the fever of the western world abated, when youth by natural reaction returned to piety, the interest in prophecy began to slip away. If we can visualize a stratigraphical chart of the American intellect, we can see this idea dropping through one social layer after another. In one decade it has largely left the academic stratum and in another it is well through that of the general educated class. Soon it is seen most conspicuously among such folk as the Mormons and the Millerites. Now and again some shred may be discerned lingering in the upper layers; one sees it in the *Essay on the Millennium* of the President of Dartmouth in 1854 and in the writings of some men of collegiate training who thought Napoleon III would probably turn out to be the Antichrist. But the course of the mass of it seems steadily downward.

It would be scientifically interesting if we could see it fall at last quite out of sight, but the end has not yet come. I extract the following announcement of a sermon from a recent issue of the *New York Times:*" . . . 8 P. M.—The Book of Revelation, the most mysterious book of the Bible; the

Book that tells of the secret coming of Christ for the Church, the political events at hand in Europe and the Near East, the rise of Iron Men like Mussolini, the revival of the Roman Empire, the coming of Antichrist as 666, the future of the Devil, the Kingdom of the Thousand Years and the Amazing Kingdom of Eternity on this Earth." This exposition doubtless took place in that city; but doubtless, also, no college presidents were present.

The academic world in general now thinks differently of the processes of nature and society. This is not because its men are abler than the men of 1800. He who reads long in the works of the scholars we have quoted realizes that they were keen and vigorous minds; but they had fewer data than their present-day successors. The Rosetta Stone, as yet unread, had not then crushed the old chronology of Archbishop Ussher; Lyell had not raised the curtain on the immense *Antiquity of Man;* modern biology had not yet brought its challenge against the separate creation theory as it did, for instance, in the *Origin of Species;* the critical apparatus of the Germans had not yet been turned against some Scripture texts themselves. The Bible as a book of science described a little intimate universe centered in the soul of man; it becomes less instructive in this aspect as the universe itself progressively enlarges.

The most distinguished American astronomer in 1800, Provost John Ewing, lecturing to his class at Pennsylvania, presented a cosmos with three thousand stars; the modern observer knows by photographic aid of thirty or forty thousand million. The horizon of man has vastly broadened, quite literally, since 1800. Dr. Samuel Latham Mitchill, at Columbia, might have read some notice of six hundred mammals; more than twenty times as many species are now known. We multiply the number of insects by five, of birds by eight, of fishes by at least fifteen, and we know that we are far from through. An American savant in 1814 ridiculed the notion that there could be twenty different snakes in the United States; to-day, surveying the domain from sea to sea, the American Museum of Natural History lists more than one hundred and fifty species. At the beginning of the nineteenth century there were two hundred minerals known to man; now there are nearly fifteen hundred. The chemical elements themselves have more than doubled. As the series is constantly filled in by new discoveries, the evidence for the theory of evolution seems steadily increased. Genesis seems less and less adequate as a book of science, whatever truth it may contain as a splendid poem.

The science of Benjamin Silliman's early days needed the Scriptural flood to account for certain phenomena: boulders transported from their geological homeland and well worn by travel, huge elephantine bones found in the north far from the tropics where, it was thought, they must have come into being. Forty days of rain could not raise a sea sufficiently to overtop the highest mountains, but men recalled the Scripture explanation that the fountains of the deep were broken up. Silliman hypothesized a cavern equal to one two-hundred-and-sixty-fifth of the earth's size and filled with water; in the profound upheaval this great bulk of water was thrown out upon the surface. The principal scientist of America draws a stupendous picture: torrents and cataracts rushing everywhere across the diminishing land to meet a tide rising on every part of the earth at a rate of over seven hundred feet each day. But then came Agassiz with his glacial theory, which accounted for boulder and beast alike, and the deluge was no longer necessary to the geologist. The flood still flows, but no longer through the pages of the *American Journal of Science*.

Rejection of the Scripture as a work of science by no means authorizes its rejection as a guide to life. As a record of religious experience, it is incomparable. It is the story of the soul of man striving to bring itself into harmony with what it apprehends to be the purpose of God; in this respect it is the

Book of Books. But Scriptural literalism, not only as to prophecy but in most other respects, has dropped out of the academic layer, at least in a large part of our country.

Count Talleyrand and other early visitors regarded the United States as a museum of culture. In the coastal cities they found habits and institutions of high civilization; somewhat to the west they came upon a less complete development; as they reached the far frontier they saw what, with some extravagance, they called barbarism. The truth is that for a long time the student of what we know as civilization, as he went west, found himself going down stairs; it is also true that the surface of the whole staircase was rising as a slowly moving stream of ideas came down from the east. But the stairs were not fixed levels; they were made up of striving human particles. Because of certain factors the new levels in the west moved upward relatively faster than the old ones in the east. If this represents American society in the nineteenth century, it is obvious that the stratigraphical chart that we imagined, some time since, becomes very complicated indeed. Our intellectual layers run straight through; to a certain extent the outcropping of the strata form the successive stairs; at any rate the lower levels are, even yet, relatively higher in the west. So the intellectual garments once cast off in

New Haven are now worn by prominent people in Tennessee and Arkansas.

The downward motion of these ideas is modified by a horizontal motion of civilization in transit, with a result for which perhaps no Isaac Newton could supply a formula. Nevertheless the primary motion of the ideas which the academic class has thrown away is downward to the point of final disappearance. Nothing could more arouse the comic spirit than to end this discourse with a brace of prophecies, yet it seems extremely likely that the idea of fundamentalism may, in the course of time, be cited as another illustration of the generalization we have stated, and it is likely too that many views and estimates of man and nature which we ourselves now dearly cherish will, in another hundred years, have followed them into oblivion.

(1)